$T\ell$

College Road
T c /bridge
r¡

the project manager

25 756260

USING PRINCE2

the project manager's guide

Paul Bradley & Melanie Franklin

Project Manager Today
P U B L I C A T I O N S

Project Manager Today Publications
Larchdrift Projects Ltd, Unit 12, Moor Place Farm, Plough Lane, Bramshill,
Hook, Hampshire RG27 0RF

First published in Great Britain 2003
Reprinted 2006, 2007

Bradley, Paul
  Using PRINCE2 : the project manager's guide
  1. Project management -- Methodology
  I. Title II. Franklin, Melanie
  658.4'04

  ISBN 978-1-900391-11-5

Printed and bound in Great Britain
by Intype Libra Limited

This book has been written for all people involved in projects whose life will hopefully be made that little bit easier by using this common-sense approach. Thanks go to our partners, Tanya and William, for their patience and support during the long hours committed by us when writing this book.

A big thank you also goes to Ken Bradley. Over the years Ken has taught, supported and helped me to cultivate a career within the PRINCE2 environment that I enjoy immensely.

Paul

I would like to thank all of the project managers, team managers and project support staff that I have the pleasure of working with, without whom project management would not be half as much fun, and from whom I continually learn valuable lessons.

Melanie

Acknowledgements

PRINCE® is a registered trademark of the Office of Government Commerce (OGC).

All PRINCE2 products published by the Office of Government Commerce (OGC) are © Crown Copyright Value Added Products which fall outside the scope of the HMSO Click Use Licence.

The reference work for the PRINCE2 methodology is the OGC publication *Managing Successful Projects with PRINCE2* (Third Edition, 2002).

OGC – the Office of Government Commerce – is an office of HM Treasury, within UK Government.

Foreword

The rapid spread and adoption of PRINCE2 has been one of the major recent developments in project management. It provides a framework for the organisation in tackling projects. It also provides a common language and understanding that can be transferred within and between organisations.

PRINCE2 can appear bureaucratic but if a method is to work there have to be 'rules of the road'. The art of using the method is in knowing which rules are important to your organisation and your projects.

This book allows a project manager with a grounding in PRINCE to see the rules in relation to the role of the project manager. I think the authors have made a valuable contribution to ensuring that PRINCE2 remains a practical tool for the project manager.

Ken Lane
Editor, Project Manager Today

Preface

This book has been written to give people involved in projects a guide on how to use the PRINCE2 methodology. The generic approach that the PRINCE2 method adopts has been maintained throughout.

Primarily aimed at project managers, the bullet-point format will help to trigger thoughts when preparing documentation and using the processes and components. This book should be used as a reference guide when managing projects, but can also be read from start to finish to give a rounded view of the PRINCE2 project management environment.

Contents

Introduction

We set out to provide a really practical approach to getting project work done, using PRINCE2. We have written it from the perspective of the project manager and it provides guidance throughout the project. It not only tells you what to do and when to do it, but, more importantly, provides ideas about how to get it done. What questions should you ask when you are checking on progress? How should you structure project meetings to make them most effective? What information should you provide to senior managers about your project? And if you are a team leader or a senior manager, we will give you a better idea of what is happening on your project.

The book is based around PRINCE2 because it is accepted throughout the UK as the leading best-practice project management approach. For many project roles, knowledge of the structure and terminology of PRINCE2 is a key requirement as it provides a common language and structure across all projects.

It is a very adaptable and flexible method for any type or size of project, is increasingly used across commerce and industry, and is at the core of most public-sector projects in local and national government, as well as police forces and the NHS.

We have divided the book into chapters, based on the different stages of the project. So, you can always turn to the most relevant chapter without having to fight your way through information you don't need right now.

PART 1 – PREPARATION

This is all about getting started and feeling prepared to run your project. It contains practical help on getting others motivated to participate in the project, as well as tips on how to structure the work so that others can participate without having to run everything past you first.

PART 2 – GETTING UNDER WAY

Before starting any project work, you need to plan the work and sort out who is going to be involved. This chapter outlines the structure for this planning and suggests the order in which it must be carried out.

PART 3 – MANAGING THE PROJECT

Once the project is up and running, progress must be closely monitored and actions taken to keep things progressing according to plan. This chapter explains how work is allocated to team members, how progress is reported, and what to do when things do not go according to plan.

PART 4 – CLOSING A PROJECT

It is important to know when you have come to the end of your project and how best to tidy up any loose ends. This chapter outlines the key priorities as the end of a project approaches and suggests how to ensure that the customer walks away satisfied with your deliverables.

All you need to do is turn to the appropriate chapter: it is not designed to be read from start to finish; just dip into the section that contains the right information for you. If you are not sure what any terms mean, don't forget to refer to the glossary and the document maps in Appendix A.

AND WHY PRINCE2?

As we said earlier, PRINCE2 is the most commonly used project management methodology, with thousands of practitioners. Its key elements are:

● Each project which is undertaken must have a stated Business Case indicating the benefits and risks of the venture and a properly defined and unique set of outcomes or products.
● For each of the products there is a corresponding set of activities to

construct them and the appropriate resources to undertake the activities.

- Projects must have an organisational structure with defined responsibilities; and a set of processes with associated techniques which will help plan and control the project and bring it to a successful conclusion.

The key benefits of using this approach are that:

- It identifies the outcomes or products that must result from the project and helps ensure that they are produced on time and to budget; as well as focusing attention on their quality
- It makes the project's progress more visible to management and gives senior management responsibility for approving progress and authorising each stage of the project
- It ensures that work progresses in the correct sequence and separates the management and specialist aspects of organisation, planning and control.

A PRINCE2 project is divided into a number of stages, each forming a distinct unit for management purposes. The delivery of products to the agreed quality standards marks the completion of the stage. A project is divided into stages based upon:

- The sequence of production of products/deliverables;
- The grouping of products into self contained sets or associated processes;
- Natural decision points for review;
- The risks and business sensitivity of the project.

It provides a structure of management controls to be applied through-out the project. They are defined at project initiation to ensure:

- The project is set up with clear terms of reference
- There are agreed and measurable objectives
- There is an adequate management structure.

These controls cover all aspects of project activity and, at the highest level, allow senior management to assess project achievement and status prior to committing further expenditure. Controls are applied through meetings of project management and project staff, with each meeting producing a set of pre-defined outputs.

Part 1

Preparation

Chapter 1

Before you start

OVERVIEW

Before starting work on any project, you will need to consider and decide on some basic principles of how you are going to work. This chapter outlines some of the key areas that should be addressed.

APPROPRIATE ACTIONS
Marketing your project

Your first vital role is the marketing of the project to all interested parties. As with any product, you will need support and buy-in from a customer base if the product is going to take off and be successful.

To gain this support, you will need to communicate regularly with everyone who will be affected by the project. Key messages will include:

- Why the project is needed. Who originated it, who from the senior management is supporting it.
- Why it is a good thing for them personally. You will need to talk to users about the things that directly affect them every day, rather than simply talking about the company.
- How the project benefits the company. What the short- and long-term benefits are, how the results of the project will position the company in terms of its customers and competitors.

In order to carry out an effective marketing campaign, you will need to survey your 'market' and find out about their special interests so that you can tailor the message to them.

Directly affected – users

We don't just mean the Senior User, who has a clearly defined role on the project. There will be a user community, comprising people who will actually use your products in the workplace.

Their concerns and interests in the project will often be at a micro level, as compared to the Senior User, who will look at the usability from a higher level.

For example, if the project is to implement a new IT system then the Senior User will be concerned that it can process the right amount of information, at the appropriate speed and with the relevant security levels. Other parts of the user community will be looking at what the screens look like, how easy it is to log on, etc.

You need to be aware of both of these levels and ensure that, throughout the life of the project, you are providing information to both parties. Ease of implementation and overall customer acceptance can often be dependent on how those in the front line perceive the project's products.

Indirectly related – other departments

Other departments may not be directly affected by the project, but there may be some concern that they might be in future, so take time to address those in close proximity to the project even if it is only to say that they should not be affected.

Informing those in support areas

A number of support functions within your organisation may wish to be kept informed of project progress so that they have an opportunity to comment on any aspects that may concern them. It is far better to identify them all up front so that they can be brought in at the relevant time.

Compliance/audit departments may have no direct input to the project, but it is useful to keep them informed (and therefore supportive) of the project. They will be concerned that the project does not introduce processes or procedures that run counter to those already in place, nor introduce new risks to the organisation.

Sources of information

When marketing your project, an excellent source of information is the Business Case. This can provide a factual base of benefits to relay to interested parties, indicating why the project is important to (a) the company; (b) their staff; (c) the way in which their departments operate.

But this is not a one-way process. In talking to the wider community, they may point out other benefits from the project. Users may identify something that can help them get a job done faster or easier. This additional information should be added to the Business Case.

The Project Board will also be a valuable source of information for the marketing campaign. Members may be helpful in addressing meetings or speaking up on behalf of the project into the wider political environment, etc. However, there is a risk that the way you market the Project will conflict with the board's expectations of the boundaries of your role, especially when speaking directly to those outside the project. Any confusion on this point should be addressed directly between yourself and the Executive very early in the project start-up.

Organising your work

This is not a book about making you a great manager; it is about running a successful project. So, this part of the book concentrates on:

a) recognising that, as the project manager, you are chief organiser and potentially your project's biggest bottleneck
    and

b) Key techniques for keeping your tasks under control:
    i. Delegation
    ii. Time management

'Information bottleneck'

The controls environment for the project, discussed in detail later in this book, is all about ensuring that information is controlled across the project, so that those requiring information have it made available to them at the right time to help them make decisions. When you are structuring your project, you need to give some consideration to how it will work on a day-to day-basis. Do all tasks and information need to be signed off by you, or are there others (including those involved in project support) that can undertake and have responsibility for the work?

How you decide to run your project will depend a great deal on how risky the project is. The more risks there are, the more likely you are going to need to be involved in every aspect. However, it is important to realise that this approach itself carries its own risks both for the project and yourself. If you retain very tight control, there will always be a queue of people waiting for you to: make decisions, give your opinion, authorise work, attend meetings and sign things off. In this situation, there is always the chance that you can turn yourself into an 'information bottleneck'. You need to be alert to the fact that waiting for you could be one of the causes of project delays although your team may not be keen to make this clear. On a personal level, this level of control gives you very little room for manoeuvre. If your absence can cause delays, you are much less likely to take time away from the project, for holidays, for thinking and strategising time, etc.

Time management

One of the joys of project management is that there are so many things to be involved in that no day is ever exactly the same as the previous one. There is constant movement towards completion with new issues emerging every day. So, it is very important that you manage the one resource which can never increase – your time. There are many books dedicated to the subject of time management, but here are a few basic principles which you can turn to whenever you are feeling pressured.

It might sound obvious, but it is important to ensure that you are spending time on the right things. It is very easy to become too involved in the detail of particular Work Packages, especially if you have experience of this work yourself, rather than concentrating on managing the project.

To keep focused, you must define the overall purpose of your role and ensure that the majority of tasks you undertake relate to this. Your overall purpose is to manage the work. Even on small projects, where you may be involved in Work Packages, you still have responsibility for the overall management. This means that you must:

● Plan the project and each stage of the project, schedule activities and create the project budget
● Define the products to be created and assign work to team members
● Assess and review progress, and take corrective action if things are not going according to plan
● Report progress to the Project Board and get their acceptance of progress and authorisation to continue
● Handle issues as they arise.

From this overall purpose, create a detailed list of activities relevant to your project and prioritise them. Identify the key areas on which you need to concentrate and delegate everything else. This will free you up for dealing with the unexpected. Once the project is up and running, use this list to help you prioritise all claims on your time as they arise.

Many project managers are very good at planning their project, but these skills are not transferred to planning their own work. It is a good idea to undertake some time planning of your own and here are some simple steps you can apply:

● Keep interruptions out of your prime time – the point in the day when you are most effective (usually mornings).
● Keep your time planning simple – work in blocks of time and do not try and allocate every minute, otherwise you will spend more time planning how to use your time effectively than actually doing it.

- Identify as many regular activities as you can and ensure they are built into the overall Project Plan and into your schedule, so that people can schedule other calls on your time around this.
- Be honest – contingency is often added into a Project Plan and you can do the same for management tasks.
- Differentiate between important and urgent tasks and treat them accordingly (see the table below).
- Important – they are relevant to the project, they keep the project moving forward.
- Urgent – time sensitive, must be carried out immediately.

Urgent but not important It is time sensitive, but try and get someone else to do it, as it is not important.	**Urgent & important** Top priority and must be done now. Takes priority over everything else.
Not important & not urgent Leave this task, or delegate it to someone else.	**Important but not urgent** Plan some time to do it.

Of course, time management is important for everyone, so it might be worth sharing this information with other members of the team. If you can encourage them to think through whether the task is either urgent, important, both of these things, or neither of them, it may well reduce the amount of work hitting your desk, and encourage them to draw your attention to urgent or important work when it arrives.

Avoid procrastination

There are many books about effective management but, as with time management, a few simple steps can get off you the starting block when faced with work you simply do not want to do.

'Work avoidance' can often have two effects:

a) it can make you very effective at doing lots of other little tasks – filing, proofreading reports, reviewing and deleting old emails. All may be very worthy in their own way, but they do not get you any closer to tackling the difficult job.

b) your preoccupation with the unwelcome task may prevent you
    from seeing past it to the wider picture of the project.

Faced with these difficulties, try the following steps:

- As in the overall project, break the tasks down into their component
  parts and assign time to each of them. This will turn the task into a
  series of small, short-term deadlines which are easier to deal with as
  they are more immediate, and you can see your way to completing
  them more easily.
- Also, by having these shorter deadlines, it should stop you
  concentrating too much on just one aspect of the task which would
  hold up the whole task.
- Visualise the benefits of completion – write them up on a wipeboard
  or on a note on your desk if it helps.
- Involve others if it will keep you motivated and focused on the task.

Delegation

It is not always easy to 'let go' and hand things over to other people, so
it is worth looking at some of the common aspects of delegating tasks.

You need to remember that, although team members may have less
experience than you in carrying out a particular task, or less experience
than is ideal, they still have the specialist knowledge to carry out the
task, and it is part of their development to take these things on.

If you are concerned that team members have the skills for the task,
but are slower than you at completing them, remember that their time
costs the company less money than yours, so getting them to do the
work at a slower pace is still an effective solution.

Early involvement in tasks, for example participating in the planning
and scoping of the work, as well as carrying out the work, can be a significant motivator for team members.

Delegation can develop experience and knowledge in team members, which might prove useful later in the project.

Part 2

Getting under way

Chapter 2

Is it worthwhile?

OVERVIEW

'Do we have a worthwhile and viable project?' This is the question that needs to be answered before any PRINCE2 project is started. The 'Starting Up A Project' (SU) process is designed to assist by providing the relevant information for an informed decision. If justification for undertaking a project cannot be provided, then there is a very good argument for not starting it.

The Project Mandate triggers projects. The PRINCE2 Manual gives a suggested outline of the Project Mandate, but it is not uncommon to find little information within the Mandate and it may not even be documented but is merely a verbal direction. A common reason for this lack of information is that the Project Mandate often comes from outside the PRINCE2 project environment.

APPROPRIATE ACTIONS
Organization

Before any work can be started, a Project Board Executive and a project manager must be appointed. These appointments are made within the first process 'SU1 – Appointing a Project Board Executive and a project manager'.

The Project Board Executive would typically be a senior manager from the business area of the organisation. He or she should have the authority to make final decisions on all aspects of the project, including financial and managerial authority.

The success of a project is largely dependent on the commitment of the Project Board members, especially the Executive, so it is good practice to appoint people who have a vested interest in the final outcome. For example, in a small company, the Executive may be the managing director or a partner. In larger organisations a departmental head may be appointed. Other Project Board members should be appointed from appropriate areas that can represent the roles properly.

The project manager is also appointed within the first process to assist with development of the Project Mandate into more detailed information. This appointment should be made carefully, with the following selection criteria being considered.

- Does the candidate have the experience required to manage the project (considering the risks and volatility forecast)?
- Does the candidate have the appropriate technical knowledge?
- Does the candidate have the credibility and respect that may be required from teams and senior managers?
- Will the project manager need softer skills – such as negotiation, persuasion and leadership, to manage teams?
- Can the candidate commit the time and effort required for the project?
- Will the candidate be available for the expected duration of the project?

The above list provides an indication of what should be asked before the appointment is made.

Diagram 1 gives outline guidance on all the roles within a PRINCE2 organisation.

When the Executive and project manager appointments have been made, thought should begin on designing and appointing the rest of the team, in particular the Senior User and Senior Supplier roles. The personnel representing these roles will bring advice to the Project Board on key interests within the project.

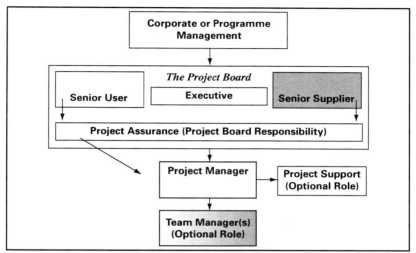

Diagram 1: The PRINCE2 standard organisation structure

The Senior User(s) should have a good knowledge of what is required from the project, and be prepared to take the responsibility for accepting all products produced from the project.

The Senior Supplier(s) must have access to specialist advice in order to represent the technical viewpoints. To gain maximum benefit from Project Board meetings the Senior Supplier/s should consult both internal and external suppliers.

A biased, unbalanced Project Board can lead to bad decisions. We can recall a project that started because the Project Board comprised two people who wanted their 'wonderful idea' implemented regardless of any adverse information. There have also been situations where 'good news' is welcome and 'bad news' is discarded. There will always be one person who is held ultimately accountable for the project delivering benefits, but other Project Board members must be interested and give support.

Designing and appointing the rest of the team should be considered at this stage. Bringing team members on board can help with ideas and other information required for the Project Brief and Project Approach.

The appointments outlined above should be considered during SU, although it is wise not to make any contractual appointments until the project has been approved.

Roles within the project management team such as Project Assurance and project support will need careful consideration. Whether the Project Board carry out their own assurance will largely depend on the scale of the project; although cost and other resource constraints often play a large part in this decision!

When considering the need for project support, it is useful to bear in mind that around 20% of a project manager's time can be saved if there is administrative help available. For example, with a project manager being charged out at £1,000 per day, and a project support function charged at £350 per day, there is a potential saving of approximately 13% costs per day.

Remember that this process is 'pre-project' when there is often little, or no, budget available. This means that the entire SU process should be carried out with an element of speed in mind. Different organisations have different ways of paying for this pre-project work. A 'slush fund' may be available for project start-up which can be repaid from the project's budget if the project is approved. Some organisations pay for project start-up from the departmental budget, charging it to the costs of running the department. Others have a general 'project slush fund' to support all projects; some organisations have nothing at all.

Project Brief

The Project Brief provides terms of reference for the project. A number of headings can be found in the templates in Appendix A. As with all templates, the headings should not be omitted. Below is an explanation of the information required.

- Background
  - Information on the source of the trigger for the work and where this project will 'fit in' to any overall strategy.

- Project Definition
  - Objectives – what will be achieved as a result of the project, as well as describing what the end product will deliver during operational life

  - Scope – what is encompassed within the project. A common technique is to draw a circle around the products required and everything inside the circle is within scope

  - Outline deliverables – details of the main products which will be developed

  - Exclusions – consider the scope of the project and clearly define what is NOT to be included as part of the project

  - Constraints – a statement of resource constraints, including time, cost and facilities available. This may include commercial or security restrictions

  - Interfaces – details of other areas of the business (or other projects) which will need to be kept informed

- Outline Business Case
  - An indication of the expected benefits that the Project could achieve. This might include high-level financial information, or a more strategic goal which assists other Projects across the organisation

- Customer's Quality Expectations
  - A brief statement on the 'level' of quality the customer is expecting. This should be balanced with the constraints on time and cost

- Acceptance Criteria
  - A definition, in measurable terms, of what must be done for the outcome of the project to be acceptable to the customer

- Known risks
  - A brief assessment of the risks associated with the project. This can be created from a generic list of project risks, along with a brief identification of specific risks

Good communication is the key to preparing the Project Brief. Remember that the SU process is intended to provide speedy information on whether a project is worthwhile. By involving the right people early on, you will be able to complete the key information in the Project Brief more easily.

The preparation of the Project Brief is the responsibility of the Project Board Executive. However, the project manager will usually produce it. The Executive must be involved when establishing the project definition so that project 'boundaries' can be established. Also, the customer will have an input, particularly when establishing the project scope, acceptance criteria and customer quality expectations.

The acceptance criteria define what criteria the end product must meet for it to be accepted at project closure. It is important to develop the criteria in discussion with the customer, otherwise you will never be sure whether the work being done is meeting them. Defining measurable criteria helps the customer establish what is wanted, and also helps the project management team establish what is required.

Meetings with the customer may be required to establish acceptance criteria. Those involved may include the user group(s) as well as the customer's management. The customer's quality expectations should also be taken into account as they need to be balanced with the constraints on the project.

Much of this information may be available from programme management: particularly the objectives and outline benefits. When identifying outline benefits, you will probably not be able to establish detailed financial information as planning and estimating are not usually undertaken till later. If the project gets the go-ahead, the costs and benefits can be expanded during initiation once there is a Project Plan. Details of the negative effects of failing to undertake the project should also be included to assist the Project Board's decision on whether to go ahead or not.

Project Approach

Decisions on how the final outcome will be delivered will need to be addressed at this point. The level of detail within the Project Approach will largely depend on information you have available.

A number of elements should be considered to ensure that the chosen approach is workable; such as quality standards (both corporate and product standards), constraints on resource available to make a particular approach viable, business impacts from the proposed approach, and whether operational support is practical once the project is closed.

Many different approaches might be possible and, in these instances, it is often good practice to run a separate project to identify the best approach.

Diagram 2 below shows two different ways of carrying this out.

The top project path demonstrates a generic approach which provides an initiation stage for the whole project, followed by the next management stage which focuses around identifying the best solution.

The lower project path shows a separate project for the 'solution' from that of the 'development'. This enables you to carry out detailed sensitivity analysis on various approaches without first having to initiate all the development stages. You should use whatever is right for you. The only advice we would give is to ensure that all parts of all projects are

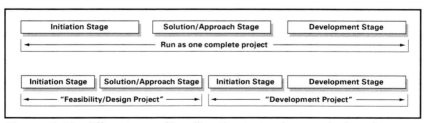

Diagram 2: The different way of handling the start and approach phase for projects

controlled under PRINCE2. We have seen some organisations control the main development project, but let any pre-work 'drift'. This is particularly common with the SU part of a PRINCE2 project. Make sure that this pre-project work is monitored and controlled – however long or short in duration.

Initiation Stage Plan

In accordance with the approach and the brief, a detailed plan for the initiation stage of the project will need to be produced. This is to establish what needs to be done, how long it will take to initiate the project, and what resources are required for 'setting up'.

REQUIRED RESOURCES

Appropriate action	Required resource	Comments
Issue Project Mandate	**Who?** • Senior management • Programme management • Board of directors • Strategy committee **What?** • Knowledge of strategy • Information from existing projects or programme.	The Mandate can come from anywhere within the corporate body. Where possible, encourage the development of key information such as benefits, time/cost constraints and interfaces before the mandate is authorised.
Appoint Executive & PM	**Who?** • Senior management	The Executive appointed should have interest in the business, rather than a biased interest in a 'favourite' product. The project manager should have knowledge of the subject matter.
Prepare Project Brief	**Who?** • Project manager – to take on the actual pulling together of the required information • Executive – Give advice to the PM on overall business strategy • Teams – Giving assistance to the PM regarding resource requirements and various approaches **What?** • Information from programme management • Software tools for planning and Business Case • Default templates and other standard information	PRINCE2 says that the Executive is responsible for the production of the Project Brief. However, it is the project manager who will be undertaking the work to prepare this information. Good negotiation and ability to pull information together are crucial. SU is often a very speedy process, and the project manager will have to use his or her skills and contacts to establish key information without taking too much time. Levels of detail need careful consideration so as not to over-do the Brief & Approach
Prepare Project Approach	**Who?** • Project manager & teams – to workshop outline approaches • Executive – Give advice to the PM on overall business strategy **What?** • Existing quality standards • Sensitivity tools to examine various approaches	The Risk Log and Business Case should be prominent at this point, as various approaches will undoubtedly affect these elements.

Chapter 3

Initiation

OVERVIEW

Having established the key information required in the Project Brief and Project Approach, further information is needed relating to the costs involved with getting the project started. In order to progress through the project in a controlled manner, you need a baseline document. This is called a Project Initiation Document (PID), and is created during the first stage of the project – the initiation stage.

For senior management to decide whether to commit resources to the initiation stage, they will need to have hard facts and figures. This is why you will need to plan the initiation stage.

APPROPRIATE ACTIONS
Why is initiation so important?

Managers in an organisation will often say: 'Why don't you just get on with it?' The answer is that without the initiation stage you will not know what you are going to do before you actually start.

Projects that get under way without a successful initiation stage will be more likely to need rework of products; are more likely to be unstructured; and are less likely to exercise the right level of control.

Applying a generic level of methodology to every project that you undertake is not good practice. You need to create baseline information that is specific to your project. In PRINCE2 this information is called the Project Initiation Document (PID).

Lack of planning the future work results in wasted effort and resources through not identifying the products to be produced and the activities required to carry out the work. Also, incorrect use of the level of controls can lead to unnecessary bureaucracy. Initiation addresses these potential problems.

Involving the right people during initiation is as equally important as the stage itself. Obtaining as accurate estimates as possible is crucial to overall costs and timescales. Also, it is essential to ensure that user and supplier provide an input to the PID so that all interests are represented and agreed.

What is in initiation?

It is within the initiation stage where you will document the following items:

- Quality
  - Quality management system
  - Acceptance criteria
  - Quality control
  - Change control
  - Configuration Management Plan

- Project Planning
  - 'Soft Project Plan'
  - Activities and scheduling
  - Identified stages

- Controls
  - Formal/informal
  - Identifying who will be involved
  - Identifying what controls are applicable

- Refining Business Case and risks
  - Add risks associated with Project Plan
  - Update costs in Business Case
    - based on plan
    - based on controls
    - based on organization

- Set-up files
  - Structure
  - Blank logs
  - Who's responsible

- Assemble PID

Quality

A Quality Management System (QMS) is a set of procedures and standards which your organization or industry must observe and meet. Those working in quality assurance are the people who create and maintain the quality system. They will be identified and will ensure that the work meets the standards.

A project management method such as PRINCE2 may be a part of the QMS. You might also have other methods and techniques identified with the QMS.

If your organization does not have a QMS, then you will need to create a temporary one for your project.

The PRINCE2 Change Control technique ensures that any changes to products or requirements are dealt with in a controlled way. You need such control to ensure that users and specialist teams alike do not change requirements and products in an ad hoc manner.

An effective change control technique will ensure that all requests for change (RFCs) and Off-Specifications are captured and analysed, and then acted upon while involving the right people at the right time. Just because it might be easier to develop something by changing the requirement slightly is not a good reason for acting without change control. This same reasoning applies to the user environment. It is within initiation that you should specify how changes will be dealt with.

In order to keep track of products and their status, configuration management must be used. The level of configuration management will differ from project to project. For instance, will all old-copy versions of documents need to be returned before new ones are issued?

If you already have a standard configuration method within your organization, you will need to discuss how your project will interface with it.

Configuration management is basically a record of every product of your project. This includes details of your specialist products, as well as your management products. Initially you will need to plan the level of configuration management that will be applied. This will primarily focus on protecting the integrity of the products. You will also need to define the relationship with the change control and filing techniques; and indicate who is responsible for operating the system. You can gather this information by:

- noting the information required for each product
  - type of product
  - version number
  - who owns the product
  - dates

- establishing how copies of products are handled and issued
  - 'signed for' when issued
  - security requirements
  - return requirements

- identifying the links and reporting processes between yourself and those maintaining the system
  - who can access products

- can teams by-pass the project manager and return products directly to the configuration librarian?
- how is the project manager informed of changes in status of products?
- reports issued for each stage to the project manager

- stating the level of audits required to ensure the configuration management system is up to date
  - How will this interface with the filing structure?

- having the links to the change control technique defined

- ascertaining who will 'own' the configuration management system after the project has closed and the products are supported in operational life.

Configuration management ensures that all products which have been approved by the Project Board, or have been signed off at quality review, will become baselined by changing the status to 'approved'. This effectively protects those products from changes by ensuring that the formal change control method is triggered when changes are required.

It is important not to try to plan your project in detail at the outset. The initiation stage is designed to establish key information for your project. Any planning carried out within Initiation should be at project level. This is a soft plan which identifies the high-level products and activities (which will be broken down into more detail as the relevant time period approaches).

Project Planning

Management stages (see Chapter 4) need to be indicated on the final Gantt plan. The key decision point, how risky the project is, and the experience of the management team, will determine this. You should also document the other controls that will be used on the project.

- How formal will communication be? (with regard to reporting and authorising work)
- Should meetings be face to face?
- Do I need formal sign-offs for all documentation?

Once this has been established, it will leave little doubt within the project team as to exactly what is required.

Business Case & Risks

An outline Business Case and Risk Log should have been created during the pre-project process 'Starting up a project'. Towards the end of the initiation stage, this information can be refined from the information from the Project Plan and controls.

By then you will have a greater understanding of costs and effort required, and also a good indication of the costs associated with the level of controls required. Also, with a clear indication of what is happening throughout the project, you will be able to remove and add risks within the Risk Log. More information is contained in Chapter 5.

Project files

You should ensure that a filing structure is created and referenced within initiation. This will outline where files are kept and who is responsible for maintaining the system. (You will find more information on the project filing structure in Chapter 5.)

The Project Initiation document (PID)

Once all the information in this chapter is complete, a master document called a Project Initiation Document (PID) is created. This is usually an assembly of all the information gathered within the initiation stage. (Chapter 5 gives more information on how to assemble and present the PID.)

Initiation Stage Plan

You will need to have the Project Brief and Project Approach close to hand. This will give you the information regarding the outline time-scales and major products of the project. You should then be able to estimate the volume of information you need to enter into your PID.

It is important that you only plan for the initiation stage. You should be identifying objectives, timescales and costs for the production of the PID – not the entire project! Remember that at this point, the project has not officially started – and may not get the go-ahead at all.

A good tip for planning and estimating the initiation stage is using a template PID that will assist you to identify the information needed for your final PID. Thinking about any standard information that can be referenced, as opposed to re-written, can considerably reduce time – and cost.

You should also speak to the people that you chosen for your management team and check their availability. You will probably need these people to help you plan the project and write your Product Descriptions. Availability will impact on your initiation stage.

PRINCE2 presumes that the 'Starting up a project (SU)' process will be a separate 'front end' to the project and approval of the initiation Stage Plan will provide authorisation for the first management stage of the project. However, for smaller, low-risk projects, the first stage might well embrace both the 'Starting up a project (SU)' and 'Initiating a project (IP)' processes.

You will need to prepare all this documentation for presentation to the Project Board. Consider the format of the initiation plan, bearing in mind that the approval could well come from an informal get-together. Reams of irrelevant information will lead to time wasting and frustration.

Presentation to senior management

Once you have completed your initiation Stage Plan you will need to get senior management approval to initiate the project. Depending on the scale of the project, this presentation could be an informal discussion, or even a phone call, or could be a full-blown formal meeting.

What you will need to ensure, however, is that all the information that was discussed in Chapter 2 accompanies your initiation Stage Plan. This should ensure that an informed decision is taken on whether to initiate the project. (More information on formal presentations to senior management can be found in Chapter 10.)

REQUIRED RESOURCES

Appropriate action	Required resource	Comments
Prepare Initiation Stage Plan	**Who?** • Project manager • Teams **What?** • Clear understanding of company requirements • Information on constraints • Team resource information	Understanding the type of project you are undertaking is important when planning the Initiation Stage Plan, as you need to think about how long initiation should take/cost balanced against the expected project life cycle. The level of information needed for your project will, of course, impact on the initiation stage. Do not be tempted to 'skip through' initiation – it is arguably the most important part of the project.
Prepare for approval	**Who?** • Project manager • Project Board **What?** • Understanding of the format required for the presentation of the plan • Presentation software for plan	The project manager should prepare appropriately for the presentation of all information from SU. This will range from an overview of initiation and the project, through to a full presentation of requirements, solutions, availability, risks & benefits; followed by presentation of the Initiation Stage Plan. In large projects, where a formal meeting will take place, the Project Board should be issued with the relevant information before the meeting. This way, discussions can take place outside the meeting – with a decision being made within the meeting.

Chapter 4

Project planning

OVERVIEW

The PRINCE2 planning principles start with a Quality Plan to establish the quality requirements and standards before planning any technical and management activities. This is a good place to start as you will need to establish whether there are any standards to work to before you start work. (The PRINCE2 outline for a Quality Plan is listed in Appendix A.)

Once quality has been established, an overall plan for the project can be created, with key stages identified. It is important to plan the work so that you can gain an idea of what will happen, when it will happen, who will be involved and using what resources.

It is worth remembering, though, that most plans are based on estimates; and estimates can be far removed from the end result! So, even with the most meticulously planned project, expect the unexpected!

APPROPRIATE ACTIONS
Quality planning

Each project that is undertaken within your organisation must observe corporate standards. These may be quality standards such as ISO 9000, a company policy or mission statement, as well as standard procedures, methods and tools.

You will need to be aware of any standards before you start planning the project. This is easier if you have a quality manual within your

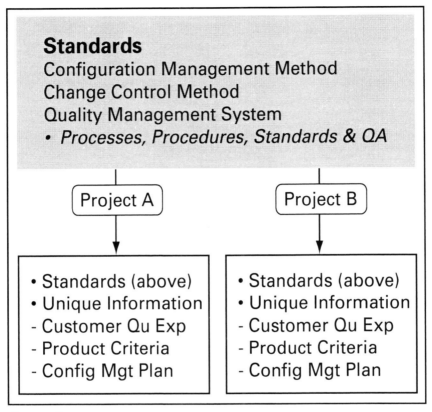

Standards
Configuration Management Method
Change Control Method
Quality Management System
• *Processes, Procedures, Standards & QA*

Project A

Project B

• Standards (above)
• Unique Information
- Customer Qu Exp
- Product Criteria
- Config Mgt Plan

• Standards (above)
• Unique Information
- Customer Qu Exp
- Product Criteria
- Config Mgt Plan

Diagram 3

organisation. If not, then you will need to talk to the projects office (if one exists) or check for any industry standards.

In Diagram 3, the quality plans for both 'Project A' and 'Project B' must include details of the QMS, change control methods and configuration management method. These are corporate standards and therefore applicable to both projects. When creating the quality plan, it is better to reference these standards rather than paste the entire standards manual into your project documentation!

You will also notice from the diagram that key information regarding each individual project needs to be incorporated into the quality plan as well. This includes the customer's quality expectations and acceptance

36 USING PRINCE2 the project manager's guide

criteria that you established in the Project Brief (see Chapter 2). The standards and criteria of key products to be produced will be included. These might include industry standards such as safety measures or certification of developers.

Staying with Diagram 3 you will see that a standard configuration management method exists. However, a Configuration Management Plan will still need to be created for each project in order to establish the level of configuration management to be used on each project. You should have discussions with the staff responsible for the corporate standards to gather advice on the flexibility of each standard. If your project does not require the 'full-force' of tight configuration management, then it would be wrong to over-cook these items just for the sake of it.

So, what happens if you do not have any corporate standards or a Quality Management System? It is fairly straightforward really – you should look to the Project Brief and ask yourself the following:

- Specifically what are the customer's quality expectations?
  - What can I do to assist with the accuracy, security & maintainability expectations?
- Acceptance criteria
  - How can I ensure the performance levels, accuracy, reliability requirements are met?
- Product requirements (quality criteria)
  - Are there any specific standards that need to be met by each of the major products that are being developed?
- Who can check it all?
  - Is there anybody who has the skills and knowledge (and independence if possible) to check that all the above is in line with the requirements?

When working with external suppliers you will need to have discussions regarding any standards that the supplier organisation needs to observe. A meeting between you, the supplier representative and, where

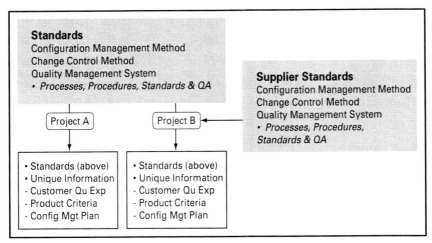

Diagram 4

possible, your own quality assurance function and that of your suppliers would be good practice to ensure that neither quality standard is compromised.

Diagram 4 demonstrates how a supplier's quality system and standards (on the right-hand side) can be incorporated into the 'Project B' quality plan. In the case of supplier standards, all information will have to be integrated so that a common understanding of quality can be established and documented.

You will also need to establish how changes will be handled. Both the user and supplier must use the specified procedure when requesting changes. PRINCE2 offers a good Change Control technique if you do not have your own. (Chapter 9 addresses more on this topic.) The important thing is to make sure that everyone is aware of how to go about asking for changes – rather than falling into the trap of team members changing things haphazardly!

Project planning

To save you wasting time trying to plan an entire project in detail at the beginning, PRINCE2 encourages you to create a 'soft' Project Plan during the initiation stage, and then to create detailed Stage Plans for each section of the project as you get there.

An example of this is a project to produce this book. It would be difficult to plan in detail the entire production, including publishing and distribution, at the 'conception' stage. It would not only have been difficult, but fairly pointless, as we all know how things change over time! Therefore, the 'soft' high-level plan created for this book identified the following major products:

- Content requirements (chapter list)
- Publication requirements & contract
- Completed draft
- Completed book (following editing and proof reading)

Product-based planning

The product-based planning technique within PRINCE2 assists with identifying the products and can be useful when further breakdowns are needed. However, in smaller projects a brainstorming session is usually adequate.

Product-based planning begins with the Product Breakdown Structure (PBS), which assists you to identify what products are needed. At project level, the PBS will identify the high-level products. You can break down to a more detailed level using the same technique to plan each stage later.

Diagram 5 (overleaf) shows the project-level products being broken down to finer detail for the Stage Plans.

Each product identified in your PBS requires a Product Description. (Headings and advice on Product Descriptions can be found at Appendix A.) You will have to be careful with the level of detailed information in your Product Descriptions. As you can imagine, producing detailed Product Descriptions for each of the products indicated in Diagram 5 would be very time consuming.

There are two different approaches when preparing Product

Diagram 5: A simple Product Breakdown Structure for a conservatory

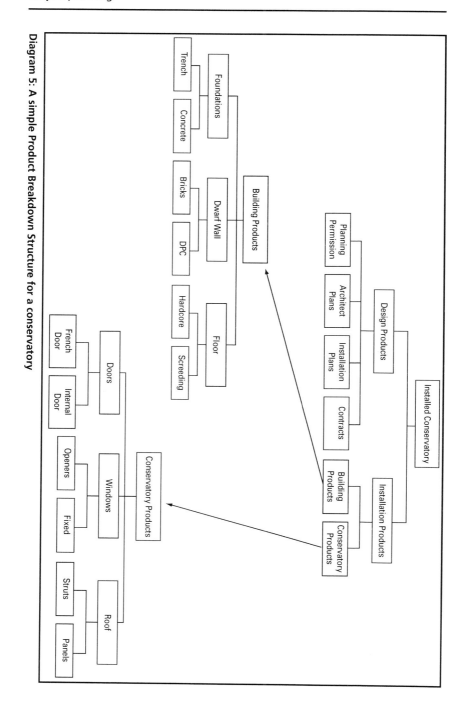

Descriptions – top down and bottom up. The top down approach will have detailed information (particularly in the composition and quality criteria sections) in the higher-level Product Descriptions. These should give enough information to ensure that your lower-level products can be developed and tested and, when complete, meet the standards required by the higher-level products. Less work is required from the project manager when writing the lower-level Product Descriptions, as the information is adequate at higher level. While teams and team managers should assist with writing all Product Descriptions, they will be more involved at the more detailed level.

You should commission the production of all management work using Work Packages. (More information on Work Packages can be found in Chapter 7.) Using Work Packages to trigger work on all management activity will ensure it is completed in time and to the right standards. Do not fall into the trap of thinking that management work can be 'fitted in' around specialist work (that applies to the project manager, too!)

The bottom up approach requires detailed Product Descriptions at the lower level. This will give greater focus on the more detailed level of work, with a general level of review at higher level. If your project-level products just require the more detailed products to be working – and working together – then this approach might be more appropriate. However, you must be sure that you are not compromising quality with either approach.

Using the advice from technical resource, and the use of the 'Derivation' heading in the Product Descriptions, you should now be in a position to create your Product Flow Diagram (PFD). The PFD shows the dependencies and relationships between your products. What needs to be planned and developed before we undertake the planning and development of another product?

Using the products from your PBS, the PFD will start with the initial products (usually requirements), and then flow in one direction until all products that require a test are represented.

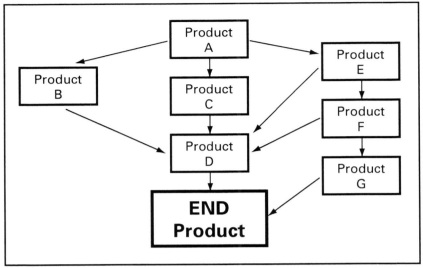

Diagram 6: Product Flow Diagram demonstrates the logical sequence and relationships of the products

Diagram 6 shows a simple example of a Product Flow Diagram. Some people actually start product-based planning with the PFD! We prefer the 'generic' way of starting with the PBS. When creating your PFD, you might find it easier to start at the bottom and work backwards. Using Diagram 6, you can ask yourself: 'What do I need in place before I develop product D?'

The reason for creating the PFD is to assist in identifying the activities that need to be undertaken. Traditionally, you might use a workshop approach and brainstorming to discover what needs to be done, as opposed to what is actually needed. This is where product-based planning is so handy. By breaking down the products you can gain a much better understanding of what is needed, and then go on to answering the question: 'What do we need to do?'

Again, you should have discussions with the teams who are going to carry out the work to establish what needs doing as opposed to a possibly 'simplistic' view of what is required. It is sometimes easier to plot the activities on the lines of the PFD. This way, you can keep a close eye on the products, too. If you identify more than, say, three to four activities between two products, then you might find that you have a product that has not been identified. You should go back to your PBS and check to see if this is the case. If it is, then you should add the new product to both diagrams.

Following all this work, you will have a list of the required products, along with a list of activities. You are now in a position to start estimating the effort and resource required to carry our each activity.

Estimating

As mentioned at the beginning of this chapter, estimating is sometimes a 'best guess'. Therefore, depending on how informed your estimates are, you will need to apply the level of contingency and control to the plan as appropriate.

The following table gives some estimating techniques. For more detailed information, you might like to search the Internet – where you will find plenty of advice!

Once the estimating has been done, your list of activities should now include durations. Diagram 7 shows a couple of standard activity planning techniques. This is a simple 'logic diagram' which shows the dependencies of each activity. Diagram 8 illustrates how, from this, you can identify activities that must be completed before others start (dependencies).

Diagram 8 shows an example of a first-sweep time network, which indicates the durations of each activity, along with the earliest and latest start and finish times, which will assist with identifying the critical path and 'float' available. You should use a software tool to complete this step of planning, although an understanding of what is happening in the background is always useful when analysing the situation.

Scheduling

Using the information on earliest start and finish times from the timed network, an earliest start Gantt plan can be produced. This

TECHNIQUE	DESCRIPTION	USAGE
Experience Lessons learned	One of the greatest sources of estimating is the knowledge of someone who has done it before.	All levels of plan Deciding on approach
Top down/bottom up	Working from the Project Plan and working down – examining stage by stage. Alternatively, estimating the individual actions within the team plans and working back to higher-level activities to be incorporated in the Stage Plans.	As appropriate according to either project or Stage Planning. Top down is useful for Project Planning. Bottom up is more relevant for Stage Planning where you can work back from the various team plans and individual plans that you already have available to you.
Function point analysis	Function point analysis presents fundamental counting techniques for basic to advanced technologies. It explains the calculations for determining function point size, an indication of a software application's overall functionality and complexity.	This method is designed for IT projects but the principles can be adapted for other types of project if required.
Delphi	Taking 1 x the best view; 1 x the worst view; and 4 x the 'middle ground' and average these out. A simple but effective technique. Adding a simple percentage to the average figure will be appropriate following the 'first sweep'.	Stage/team plans

chart will provide the basis for Project Board approval (Diagram 9).

The timed network will have assumed unlimited resources were available and concentrated solely on the underlying logic of the relationship between activities. This does not, of course, mean that any number of people are available to the project, but that those that are assigned to the

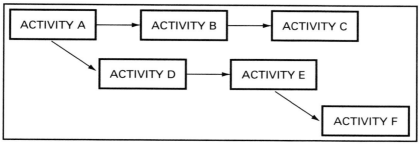

Diagram 7: Logic diagram

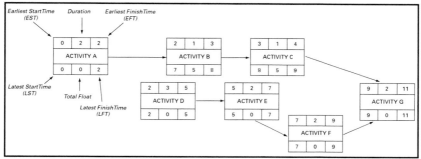

Diagram 8: Planning network

project are assumed to be able to work at any time (even to the extent of carrying out simultaneous, multiple activities).

You will need to consider the resources that you have available and, where necessary, 'level' the plan to make it more realistic. There is no point in submitting plans showing over-optimistic scheduling. A more realistic plan will be easier to present to the Project Board when explaining the assumptions you have based your plan on. Many software tools have a facility for 'smoothing' the plan according to resources available. This makes the job less tedious – but do make sure you save the file before hitting the button!

Once you have created your Project Plan showing the overall project activities, you should identify the management stages which show the key points where the Project Board need to make decisions. These decision points usually fall naturally in line with the completion or start of major activity. You should also consider the products being produced

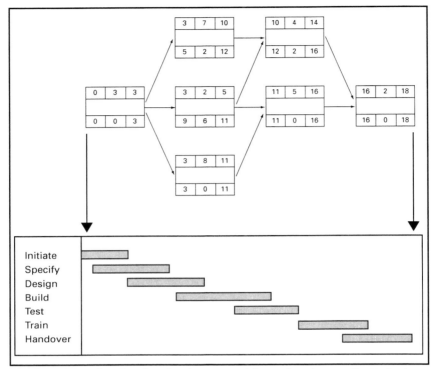

Diagram 9: Transforming the planning network into a bar chart or Gantt chart

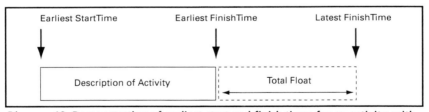

Diagram 10: Demonstration of earliest start and finish times for an activity, with total 'float' available indicated

from the activity to assist you with identifying these stages. (Chapter 5 explains in more detail the use of stages and how to handle the crucial time between them.)

Presentation formats

In order to assist you with presenting your plan, you should consider using a resource report. Diagram 11 shows a template produced by a software tool. This will provide the Project Board with clear information on what they are committing to at any one time.

The example breaks down the different cost elements which include effort, costs and facilities. A clear indication of planned and actual will assist with the decision when plan approval is required.

Other examples of easy-to-view information include graphical summary and earned value analysis (EVA). EVA enables a clear measurement of the project work accomplished . The value is usually monetary but can be expressed in any appropriate unit such as staff hours or days (see Diagram 12). The value to be earned when a specific milestone or major product is achieved is based on the planned cost of achieving the milestone.

For example, if the plan showed that £100,000 was required to achieve a specified milestone/project product, £100,000 worth of earned value would be credited to the project manager (as 'owner' of the product) when achievement of the product was demonstrated (ie,

	Stage 1		Stage 2		Stage 3	
	Plan	*Actual*	*Plan*	*Actual*	*Plan*	*Actual*
EFFORT (Staff Weeks)						
SKILL TYPES						
Customers						
Engineers						
IT Staff						
Other Staff						
COSTS (£'000)						
SKILL TYPES						
Customers						
Engineers						
IT Staff						
Other Staff						
Equipment						
Fixed Price Elements						
Total Stage Costs						
Total Project Costs						

Diagram 11: Tabular resource report

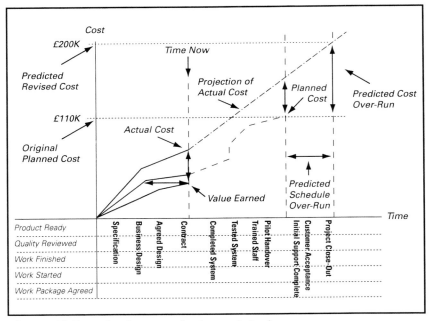

Diagram 12: Example of an earned value analysis plan

that the product had successfully met all its quality criteria). It is worth emphasising that the techniques described above are not requirements of PRINCE2, but are useful vehicles for illustrating project situations to the Project Board and other senior managers.

When presenting a bar or Gantt chart to the Project Board, try to get the entire plan on one page. We have lost count of how many plans we have seen that have dozens of pieces of paper with just one activity line spanning from the left-hand side of the page to the right!

REQUIRED RESOURCES

Appropriate action	Required resource	Comments

Project Quality Plan	**Who?**
	• Project manager
	• Team manager
	• Quality manager/Quality Assurance
	• Project Support Office
	• Suppliers
	What?
	• Customer's quality expectations
	• Project Approach
	• Quality manual
	  ° Processes
	  ° Procedures
	• Company standards
	  ° Configuration management
	  ° Change control
	  ° Filing structures
	• Industry standards
		The customer's input is essential when establishing quality. Your objective is to meet the customer's quality expectations. Involve the customer when planning quality.
		You need to know what standards are to be met. You can establish this information from your company quality manual (if there is one). This will give details of standards, processes and procedures. The quality assurance function can help you define how to apply that quality to your project. Also, where you have identified external suppliers, make sure that they give you information of their own quality standards that need to be met. You can plan with this in mind.

Project Plan	**Who?**
	• Project manager
	• Team manager
	• Project Board
	What?
	• Experience/knowledge
	• Planning tools
		The project manager is responsible for planning the project. However, teams should assist – particularly with writing Product Descriptions and estimating.
		The Project Board should be involved when deciding on management stages.
		    • How much are they prepared to commit at any one time?
		    • Format required for presentations?
		
		Check for standard planning & estimating tools that should be used (ie, MS Project, Primavera, Welcom, Artemis, etc.)

Chapter 5

Setting up the project

OVERVIEW

During initiation, you will need to set up the project. This will include establishing the level of controls to be applied and the filing structure that will be used. Also, the impacts of the Project Plan and control structure on the Business Case and Risk Log should be demonstrated. This chapter explains what should be considered when undertaking this important part of the project.

APPROPRIATE ACTIONS
Project controls

In order to assist with the delivery of a successful project, you will need to use a level of controls as appropriate.

PRINCE2 offers many different controls. The various controls are largely discussed in Part 3 – Managing the project. This chapter focuses on deciding the level and types of controls you are planning for your project.

There are a number of questions to be answered in order to determine the level of controls that should be applied on your project:

- Has this type of project been run before?
  - Standard in-house project
  - Do I have access to previous project files?
- Have I run this type of project before?
  - What technical support from the teams do I have?

- Skills available (technical/management/soft skills)
- How accurately can the estimating be done?
  - Can tolerance be negotiated?

- What is the level of risk associated with this project?
  - Low risk – longer stages
    - How far ahead am I able to realistically plan in detail?
    - Stages at key decision points
    - Can a stage be planned for longer durations?
    - Should I plan in detail further than three months, anyway?
    - How far can I plan without increasing risks?
    - Increases and encourages 'management by exception'

  - High risk – shorter stages
    - Less commitment at any one time
    - Higher Project Board Involvement

- Is the Project Board prepared to accept high risk?
  - What is the board's level of involvement?
  - High benefit – high risk

- Do I have direct contact with the teams?
  - Are the teams my own staff?
  - What are the line managers' interests?
    - Communication between project and line management

- How many sites are involved?
  - Communication between sites
  - Across how many countries?
    - Do we need meetings or tele-conferencing?

- Are the suppliers internal or external to this organization?
  - What is the relationship with suppliers?

    ◦ What was Executive's view on organization structure?

● Have we used the suppliers before?
  • What was delivered?
    ◦ How was it delivered?

● Are contractual arrangements required?
  • ITT
  • Preferred supplier

The main areas to consider are:

● Risk & stages
  • Number of decision points
  • Representation of Project Board members

● Geographical location
  • Communication
  • External suppliers

Risk and Stages

When considering risk, you will need firstly to revisit the frequency of your management stages. To react to high-risk projects, the use of shorter management stages can be adopted. This will reduce the level of firm-commitment risk at any one time.

Diagram 13 overleaf demonstrates that the firm commitment given by senior management is for the stage that immediately follows the management meeting. This means that the resources approved are for that time only, with an 'in principle' approval for the rest of the project. Identifying shorter management stages gives the following benefits:

● Project Board has more control
  • Reduction of level of financial commitment

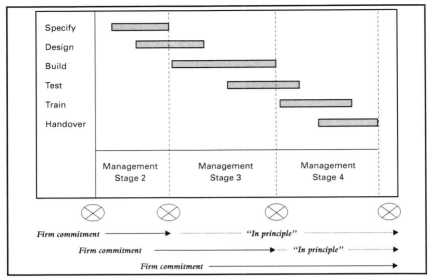

Diagram 13: Commitment of resource for each stage of the project

- Involvement through more end-stage assessments (ESAs)

- Project manager has shorter timescale to manage
  - Simpler plans
  - Easier monitoring of overall stage
  - Fewer activities/products to manage per stage

Of course, the shorter the management stages, the more time the Project Board needs to commit to meetings (ESAs). Also, the project manager will need to produce more reports at the end of each of the stages, and more time will be needed by the project manager and teams to arrange planning sessions to create the detailed Stage Plans. This all leads to the balance of high-level controls against the time and costs of exercising them.

When considering the format for management meetings, you should speak to the Project Board to determine their availability for, and the formality of, the ESAs.

There is a need to consider whether to have:

- formal or informal meetings with all Project Board members attending
- formal or informal meetings with representatives for Project Board members
- telephone conferencing between Project Board members
- virtual meetings with representations
- verbal communication between Executive and project manager

You will also need to decide on how the stage ends will be handled. What happens if the Project Board members cannot be available to give authorisation for the next stage? You would not want your resources idle.

Diagram 14 gives a suggested way to handle the situation where Project Board members are not available to meet at the end of a stage. You will see that work due to be carried out in the next stage has started before the end-stage assessment has been held. This approach can be used providing that the work carried out 'in between' the management stages has been identified as high risk. It needs to be understood that, in the pure PRINCE2 environment, you must never have work undertak-

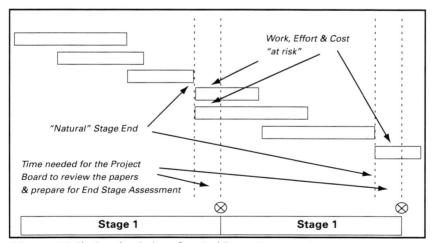

Diagram 14: Flexing the timing of an End Stage Assessment

en without authorization; and management stages must never overlap.

However, there will be times when common sense needs to prevail. When adopting the above approach, you should at least have a discussion with the Project Board Executive to advise him or her of what is happening and to give your opinion on the situation of this 'unauthorised' work.

The activity that has been identified as 'high risk' is still being controlled in the PRINCE2 fashion!

Geographical location

When your project spans multiple sites, you will need to consider the interfaces between each of the sites. Will you need face-to-face meetings with the teams or can you confidently manage them remotely?

Again, you will need to consider the costs of face-to-face meetings and whether value for money is achieved. Perhaps a compromise can be made by increasing reporting periods and having fewer meetings.

If you are working across multiple locations, consider if you need to meet with team managers to hand over Work Packages. Is it possible to simply document all your requirements and follow up with a telephone call to minimise costs?

Think about the close links between Senior Supplier and teams in an external supplier situation. With the Senior Supplier having assurance responsibilities, it is a good idea to forge links with this role to address any potential shortfalls in communication. Where close links between the project management team are required, but costs are tight and distance is far, then this might be a workable solution. It does however mean that a Project Board member would be reporting to you(!) but given the right spin, it could just work!

You should make use of IT as well. Collaborative working tools on the Web or Intranet can provide ways for geographically dispersed teams to communicate. Consider creating an area on the Intranet that gives updates to all involved (message boards, etc).

Setting up files and logs

It is now time to plan the organisation of the project documentation. You need to understand what records you need to keep, and where and how documents should be stored. It is no good, halfway through the project, identifying records you should have been keeping when you can no longer remember exactly who said what and when. It is easier to be organised from the start, as you will feel more confident in your ability to handle things if you can always find the document you want when you need it most.

Some of the information set out below may look like overkill, but just use the points that are relevant for your project. It may look like a lot of administrative work but it will pay dividends later, as there will be:

- less problems finding relevant information
- less frustration dealing with inconsistent format of deliverables
- no need to do rework on work that has already been completed

To get organised, you need to carry out the following actions:

- create the structure and hierarchy for your filing system
- decide on the naming conventions and formatting for all project documents
- identify how information will be stored and who can have access to it
- create logs to record details of any Project Issues and note any useful lessons learned as the project progresses
- create document templates

Create the structure and hierarchy for your filing system

There is a risk that this can become over-complicated and over-engineered. The key to a good filing structure is that there is a place for everything, and that the structure is intuitive; there should be no need to agonise over where something should be stored – name the files with obvious, simple titles using familiar terminology. It will save hours of hunting later.

If you are worried about things becoming complicated, set out some ground rules to help team members identify the document type. For instance, if you are going to have a project file and files for each stage of the project, clearly state when something relates to the project as a whole rather than the stage that document was created in.

Structure

Whatever approach to filing you use, three main areas of work need to be covered:

- management of the project
- details of the projects deliverables
- records of quality activities throughout the life of the project

Suggested filing structure

Establish an overall project file, and separate files for each stage of the project. The advantage of this structure is that the project manager can retain control of the information. External suppliers can be responsible for maintaining an individual stage file but the project manager can prevent access to the overall project file. Another advantage is that, even on small projects, the overall project file can become very large.

Decide on the naming conventions and formatting for all project documents and suggested naming conventions. Identify a naming convention for authors of project documentation to follow. This way, it will be much easier to identify documents going forward. Key issues to consider are:

- What should the document name contain?
  - Name
  - Date
  - Version number
  - Author identification

- In what format should each piece of information be held?
  - Date format
    YYMMDD or YYYYMMDD?
  - Document name
    - Should the name include phrases which will identify the status of the document such as: draft, work in progress, final, internal use, external use?

- Keywords/indexing
  - When documents are saved, should keywords be used to help search for them at a later date? If so, make sure every author is aware of this before documents are created, otherwise you will waste time performing a keyword search for documents with no keywords.

- Allocating reference numbers
  - When creating reference numbers, it might help to start them with a code which identifies what the number refers to. For example, issues, quality checks and risks all require a unique reference number to be recorded against them in the Issues Log, Quality Log and Risk Log respectively. Therefore, as an example, their reference numbers might start as: ISS001; RSK001; QC001.

Formatting

Agree with team members a standard approach to formatting documents. This will give all documents a standard look and feel, irrespective of who has created them. Key items to consider are:

- font
- font size
- use of contents and index pages
- use of logos, their size and positioning
- use of title pages

- standard content of headers and footers
- page numbering conventions
- use of appendices

Note: In large corporations the corporate communications department may have a standard format that all documents should follow. Sometimes these rules only apply to documents that are external to the company, but they might give you some ideas.

Identify how information will be stored and who can have access to it. Give consideration to who will need information and in what form (use your Communication Plan to understand all of the participants to the project). From this assessment, you can plan where information will be held and how it can be accessed. Points to consider are:

- Intranet site with current versions of documents available for public access
- network access, password controlled

Create logs to record details of any Project Issues and note any useful lessons learned as the project progresses. It is a good idea to create any logs while you are still planning and setting up the project; you can then capture relevant information as soon as it arises.

Issues log

This will be a key document for monitoring and controlling the project on a day-to-day basis. Therefore, make sure it is as user friendly as possible. You will want to take information from this log to use as the basis for any Exception Reports as well as including overviews in highlight reports and presentations to Project Board members. It will also be reviewed regularly by Project Assurance.

Consider how you will sort the information to provide the reports that you need. Also think about how each issue will be indexed and what the numbering convention should be.

You may also want to sort by type or priority or by who the issue has been assigned to.

Consider how to present the data, as there is a lot of information on the log – how best can it be printed and does it all fit on one page?

Quality Log

This log summarises all the quality checks that are planned or that have already taken place. As each quality check is logged, it will be assigned a unique reference number. This first entry is made when the quality check is entered onto the Stage Plan. All remaining information will be added each time the check is performed.

Lessons Learned Log

In PRINCE2 the purpose of the Lessons Learned Log is to be a repository of any lessons learned during the project in order to provide useful information for future projects of a similar nature.

It is important to keep the structure of this log very simple and straightforward. There will be a time for categorising lessons and formatting the information when the Lessons Learned Report is produced during 'Closing a project'.

Create document templates

For documents that are going to be created regularly it is worth designing and setting up a simple template. This means that the creation of the documents can be delegated to other team members without having to worry about what the finished product will look like.

Consider creating templates for:

- agendas
- minutes
- slide presentations
- reports (Highlight Reports, Checkpoint Reports, Exception Reports)
- Issue form
- Change request form

Software

Filing structures are more complex for bigger projects, especially if external people need access to the documents. It is likely that you will be using software to manage the filing rather than simply keeping hard copies. It might sound obvious but identify early on any incompatible software between team members and agree an approach. There are some key questions to address:

- Are all project participants going to be using the same word processing, spreadsheet and presentation software?
- Are all project participants on the same versions or releases of the software?
- Can external people have permission for network access?
- Can they dial in to your network from their offices?
- Are there any rules operating with your email system that prevent documents being sent to external addresses?
- Will document-naming conventions be compatible globally?
- Could you use collaboration software?

Back-ups

Ensure the frequency of back-ups is in line with the pace of the project. For complex projects with multiple issues, risks and complex stage and team plans, back-ups should be performed frequently. Look at how much information is created and changed on your project each day, to ascertain whether daily or weekly back-ups are most appropriate. Also, consider the process for performing back-ups. If it is cumbersome and time consuming, this must be balanced against the value gained from having copies of up-to-the-minute documents.

Document management software

If document management software is used in your company it may help to resolve some of the issues raised above, as the software usually comes with a standard logical structure. However, make sure each member of your team knows how to use it, and what the various rules and conventions are for saving and updating information.

Refining costs, benefits and risks

Once you have prepared the Project Plan and are comfortable with the estimated costs and timescales, you can think about fine-tuning the Business Case. You will need to bring in the information gathered from the initiation stage in order to make the costs and benefits more tangible.

Benefits

You will probably find that you will be required to put a costing to all the benefits that have been identified. If, for instance, you are outlining intangible benefits such as 'easier to use' or 'happier staff', then you should try to cost them. The following are examples of the thought process you might adopt:

- 'Happier staff'
  - lower staff turnover
    - reduces recruitment costs
    - reduces training costs
      - review annual costs
      - estimate % savings
        - apply cost savings

- 'Easier to use'
  - encourages use
  - improves process
    - increases productivity
    - more cost-effective
      - by how much?
      - hours rate per head

Indicating a cost element to benefits will not only help to assist the

Project Board to make informed decisions on whether the project is viable, but will also help you to prioritise benefits.

You should be working closely with the Executive at this point to establish whether there are other benefits and costs from other areas of the organisation. It could be that other people and divisions might use, or be affected by, the products being produced. If this is the case, then all this information should be documented in the Business Case. Be sure to check with the Executive for this.

Once you have identified and costed all the benefits that your project is expected to bring, you can carry out analysis on the Business Case to identify which benefits the project is most heavily relying on. This is known as sensitivity analysis. If you know what benefits are of most importance, then you can ensure that steps are taken to protect that part of the Business Case. You might need to address risks in a different way, or ensure that all interested parties are aware of the key elements of the project contributing to these benefits.

Costs

Using your Project Plan, along with other information from your teams, you should be gathering a better idea of costs. You should examine each stage that has been identified on the Project Plan, break down the costs, and then work them back to give you a greater idea of management and development costs.

The controls that you have planned will need to be considered, too. Where controls have been made more formal, then costs will be pushed up. If you have decided to have meetings for all checkpoints, highlights and management matters, there will be costs such as travel and attendees' time.

Additional organisational costs will need to be applied where Project Board members have appointed a Project Assurance function or a Change Authority to act on their behalf.

To bring these various elements together, you should involve somebody from Finance to assist you with completing the Business Case.

When you are establishing how each benefit will perform over a period of time, you should consider the cost of tying up the cost of the project funds. A costs–benefits analysis/investment appraisal is a simple way to demonstrate the projected benefits over a period of time. This will give information on:

- the costs over a period of time
- the expected benefits
- the cash flow (benefits added onto costs)
- a discount factor applied to the cash flow (representing other investments that could have been made with the capital)
- a final cumulative 'discounted cash flow' figure, year on year

Of course, this information will arguably be the most volatile information within your project. As slippages occur, costs increase, risks may increase, and benefits fall. Do use a software tool to keep track of this information, and do keep a very close eye on things!

Many companies prefer to keep the Business Case out of the Project Initiation Document for commercial reasons. Remember that, by default, all the project management team has access to the PID, and therefore access to the financial information contained within the Business Case. Think carefully about this.

Risks

Management of risk within PRINCE2 consists of several steps:

- Identify the risk
- Assess probability and impact
- Assign an 'owner'
- Decide on actions
- Evaluate the cost of actions against cost of risk occurring
- Plan activities to carry out the actions
- Ensure the actions are working

You will have created the Risk Log in the SU process. You will need to update that Risk Log now that you have more information. As a result of creating your Project Plan and deciding the way forward, some risks that had been identified earlier will have become irrelevant. However, you will no doubt have identified new risks from the plan. These might include:

- low customer or staff involvement expected and little contribution
- staff have many other responsibilities
- there is a dependence on development facilities which are outside the control of the project team
- significant impact on business as usual by the project
- approximations have been used based on unreliable estimates

To help you identify the risks that now face your project, you may need to hold a risk workshop with the teams. Areas to look for are threats to:

- the plan being achieved
- resource availability
- specified requirements (Product Descriptions)
  - understanding the requirements
- product delivery times
- the Business Case (costs)
- compatibility of products

These are just a few things to consider. During the risk workshop, each risk should be entered in the Risk Log, and evaluated to assess the probability and impact of each risk. Undertaking the evaluation during the workshop will avoid having to meet again unnecessarily.

If you can establish the full list of risks, with details of their importance, and actions identified, then you will be in a position to evaluate the cost of the actions against the cost of the risk occurring.

Risks actions that will be undertaken will need to be planned. You should incorporate the activities into your Stage Plan so that you can resource and delegate them. Management activities can be delegated to the relevant resources using Work Packages when appropriate. Do be careful not to overdo this type of control.

Throughout the life of the project, risks will come and go. When a risk becomes an issue, the issue process will kick in (see Chapter 9). Also, if the status of a risk exceeds any agreed risk tolerance, you will need to follow the exception procedures.

As new risks are identified and other risks diminish, you will need to keep the Risk Log up to date. The Risk Log can become very detailed and difficult to read. When presenting a summary of the risk situation to the Project Board, you might like to use a more graphical indication.

Diagram 15 shows that risks 1, 2 and 5 are within tolerance (represented by the thick line). There is also an indication of the level of management being applied to each of these risks. Risk 6 is above the tolerance line and therefore requires escalation. Amber indicates that risk management is being used significantly on this risk, as with risk num-

High Probability (scores 3)		3 (Green)	
Medium Probability (scores 2)		4 (Red)	
Low Probability (scores 1)	2 (Green) 5 (Green)	1 (Green)	6 (Amber)
	1 *(Very Low Risk)* Impact	**2** *(Low Risk)* Impact	**3** *(Moderate Risk)* Impact

Diagram 15: Risk profile indicating status of each risk associated with the project

ber 4 in the table. However, the real concern here is risk number 3. This risk is clearly above the tolerance line and the level of management being applied to the risk is low (green).

This type of summary makes it easier for both the project manager and Project Board to fully understand the situation at a glance.

REQUIRED RESOURCES

Appropriate action	Required resource	Comments
Setting up project controls	**Who?** • Project manager • Project Board • Programme management • Contracts management **What?** • Contract Information • Programme plan ∘ Controls	Consider the approach and look at the suppliers that will be used. Do you already have contracts with the suppliers, and if so, what is in those contracts that will impact on your controls? You need to think carefully about the cost of applying formal controls (budget and time). Speak to the Project Board to find out the level of control that they expect.
Setting up project files	**Who?** • Project manager • Project support **What?** • Allocated system space • DMS software • Template documents	You must have a filing system in place to hold products in a structured way. Don't wait until 'IP5' within the method to set this up. The filing structure should be one of the first activities you do. Use standard forms and templates for consistency and speed.

Refining Business Case & risks	**Who?**
	• Project manager
	• Executive
	• Finance representative
	What?
	• Project Plan
	• Controls information
	• Programme Risk Log
	• Project timescales
	• Project costs
	  ∘ Technical
	    • Development
	  ∘ Management
	    • Controls
	• Resources report
		When adding information to these products, careful thought should be given to all costs associated with the project. This will include not only the development costs, but also the costs of management activity and facilities. Both products will be updates of the initial information that should have been created in SU. The Executive should be involved at all times as he/she will be ultimately responsible for both.

Chapter 6

Documenting the project

OVERVIEW

The Project Initiation Document is the focal point for all information relating to the what, why, who, how and when of the project. It is used as guidance and information for all those involved. It provides a basis on which the project can be authorised and on which other management decisions need to made during the life of the project.

The key issue is that the PID is assembled, not written. You already have the content produced as a result of all the start-up and initiation tasks. Therefore, you should concentrate on structuring the document so that all the important information is included; that it is in the most appropriate order for your project, and that the document is actually readable. It must not be so cumbersome that the reader would need to book a week off work to get to grips with it.

The PID can become a large document with very detailed information about the project. It is important to consider how best to present it. All the information is relevant to the management of the project and, in an ideal world, every recipient would read it thoroughly. However, in the real world it's unlikely that senior management will have the requisite time.

Review each piece of information and see if it would be better held in an appendix, so that the main document remains user friendly (ie, a handful of pages and diagrams),

APPROPRIATE ACTIONS
Assembling the Project Initiation Document

Even if you are not a great documenter, there are some important steps needed to ensure that the PID forms part of 'involved decision making' so that people really do understand the issues on which they are agreeing, and consequently are less likely to change their minds later on.

To get organised, you need to carry out the following actions:

- Identify the audience for the PID
- Decide on the structure of the document
- Decide how the information should be held
- Gather all the project documentation created so far
- Add any narrative or explanatory text
- Submit the PID to the Project Board for review and authorisation

Identify the audience for the PID

It is important to have a brainstorming session with all those who might have an interest in reading the PID (or sections of it) and to understand how they will be using the document. Until you have done this there is no point trying to assemble the document. Your thoughts from this step should help you decide on what are the key pieces of information, and what your audience might regard as 'nice to haves'. From this you can work out how to order the document (see table opposite).

Decide on the structure of the document

Make sure that the document is structured in the most 'user friendly' manner, thereby avoiding a stream of complaints about the amount people are asked to read.

Consider dividing the PID into a number of referenced chapters or sections, and make it easy to navigate. Give them some easy to understand navigation of the document. Create a navigation page for large or complex documents. This is often a flow diagram of some sort, with dif-

Key audience members	Areas of interest and/or concern
Project Board	As a decision-making body, the members will authorise the PID and therefore commit to the plans and resources specified within it. However, each member of the Project Board will have a specific area of interest: it is worth reviewing these to ensure you are providing all the necessary information.
Senior User	As the Senior User represents those that who be affected by the final outcome of the project, the project definition and the quality expectations will be of particular importance. All the information in these sections must be written with the full involvement of the Senior User or their representatives. The timescale for interim deliverables and the completed project are key issues for the Senior User.
Senior Supplier	The Senior Supplier needs fully to understand exactly what is required so the project definition/terms of reference are important. The Senior Supplier is responsible for committing technical resources to the project, and the scheduling of these resources will be of prime interest; so the resource plan is important.
Executive	The main focus for the Executive will be the Business Case. Whatever the project is planned to achieve, there must be a clear statement of benefits. To balance this, there must be a statement of the costs and the risks associated with achieving these benefits. The Business Case, more than any other, enables the Executive to give his or her authorisation, as the Executive is committing resources (people, time and money) based on the promise of future benefits. Another potential area of interest for the Executive will be the controls used to manage the project on a day-to-day basis.
Project Assurance	One of the first things that Project Assurance will look for will be a clear statement of the roles and responsibilities across the project organisation. This is to ensure that all key activities will be covered.
Departmental heads/ line managers	Those who are affected by the project, either because they will be expected to supply resources, or because the project team will be operating in their area, will be interested to see when these 'disruptions' are scheduled to take place. Another area in which they might be interested includes the budget (money spent on your project).

ferent colours to indicate different sections. The flow diagram helps readers understand how the different sections relate to each other and where in the document they can be found.

As we said earlier, you can use appendices to hold detailed information. This could include, for example:

- job descriptions (only the organisation structure diagram appears in the main body of the PID)
- detailed Product Descriptions, estimates and scheduling diagrams (eg, network diagrams).
  The Gantt chart can best illustrate the Project Plan so that is all that needs to appear in the main body. However, to help navigate through the document, milestones can be drawn on the Gantt chart for completion of each product, with a reference to the pages where the relevant Product Descriptions can be found.

Decide how the information should be held

The PID will be used for ongoing comparison of project progress against plans. It should be easy to access, so the first decision is the format of the hard copy of the document. Obviously, for something so important, there will be a soft copy, which can be distributed via email. However, the hard copy of the original will be needed for reference, and the project manager will use it when briefing people on the project as well as when planning each stage.

As there are three volatile parts to the PID, consider using a ring binder, so that the updated versions of the Project Plan, Business Case and Risk Log can easily be inserted. Otherwise, complete bound copies will have to be reproduced each time any of them are changed.

Gather all the project documentation created so far

The PID consists of all project documentation created during start-up and initiation. These documents should be gathered together, and it may be worthwhile reviewing them for consistency of approach, use of terminology, etc, so that the document has integrity.

Add any narrative or explanatory text

Each of the documents collected above will make sense in its own right. However, you might need to add some kind of executive summary to the front of the PID, just to explain the overall purpose, as well as adding text to each of the documents to explain how they relate to each other.

Submit the PID to the Project Board for review and authorisation

Once the PID has been assembled, it requires authorisation before the project can move to the next stage. The Project Board and other interested parties must be given sufficient time to review the document. It is risky to assume that any points can be resolved as late as the end-stage assessment.

Presenting the Project Initiation Document to senior management

Once the PID has been assembled and reviewed, it needs to be authorised by the Project Board at a formal meeting. Within PRINCE2 this formal meeting is called an End Stage Assessment. The purpose of the End Stage Assessment is to:

- gain authorisation for the PID
- gain authorisation for the next Stage Plan

Even if the document has been well received during its review, gaining a formal commitment is not always straightforward. It is your job to help the Project Board make the leap from being happy with a document to saying yes to the commitment of time, money and resources.

A number of common problems are likely to arise. For instance, if the Project Board will not give approval to the PID immediately because:

- there is so much information in the PID that they feel they need more time to review it and therefore postpone the End Stage Assessment

- they feel that the information it contains must be reviewed by a wider audience
- they want to see very low-level details and plans about a specific aspect before committing resources

To mitigate the risk of such delays occurring, it is important to show clearly how the approval of the PID and next Stage Plan link to the initial activities, and make it clear in the plan text exactly what the knock-on effects of delays are going to be. The effects of these delays could include staff sitting idle, risk of supplier costs escalating, etc. Also, knowing that a delay is a very real risk to your project, you should tackle it just like any other risk. Identify actions that reduce its probability. For example:

- Take the Executive through the PID in advance of the meeting to get his/her support. The Project Board is not a democracy and you will always need the support of the Executive to get any authorisation. Executives do not like surprises or to be made to look foolish, so make sure they are fully informed and briefed before the end-stage assessment.
- Identify key items within the PID on which you would like specific authorisation so this will give the meeting a useful structure. After all, you need the Project Board to actively engage with the PID so that their sign-off has meaning. If you draw their attention to specific areas and take them through the information, it is going to be much harder for them to backtrack on their authorisation later on by claiming that they had not noticed nor understood the ramifications of a particular area.
- Produce a list of suggested criteria or key points from the PID that must be specifically signed off by the Project Board. This is a helpful ploy as it focuses the review effort and gives it a clear end point.
- Arrange meetings with departments or teams who will be affected by, or have an involvement in, the project. Go through the Project Plan with them and obtain signed confirmation that they are happy to

participate. This stops the Project Board holding up agreement by widening the distribution of the document — you have already taken care of it and obtained approvals to prove it!

- As part of the PID, there will be detailed roles and responsibilities attached to the proposed organisation structure. As a precaution, go through these descriptions, not only with the people proposed for the role, but also their line managers and HR. Also get confirmation from line managers and HR that the proposed team members can be released from their existing work.
- The Communications Plan will usefully state not just what and who, but also how communications are to be structured. In a large organisation you should ensure that your corporate communications department is happy with your schedule of internal communications and that it does not conflict with its plans.
- The Project Approach will set out how the project will be delivered. Ensure that the practical application of the approach has been checked with affected departments and that no one is unhappy with the approach. If they are they may notify the Project Board, which could delay authorisation.

A general tip for speeding up approval of the PID is to identify all potential 'hot spots' that concern or involve different members of the Project Board. Allay their concerns by showing that you have consulted and reviewed with all relevant parties who are happy with what you have written. Make it as easy as possible for the Project Board member to say 'Yes'.

If there is something in the PID with which one of the Project Board, or their staff, are expert, ensure that they have been given an advance copy for their input, or discuss the issue ahead of the End Stage Assessment. In this way you can generate their support or have time to undertake any follow-up actions that they might suggest before the End Stage Assessment, so that there is no reason to fail to obtain authorisation at the End Stage Assessment.

Suggested presentation elements

When producing the documents for the meeting, think about key elements that should be formally presented to the Project Board, and the best ways of presenting them. Suggest any changes that should be made to the documentation for presentation purposes (detail that can be glossed over).

Timings and agenda

However short the presentation, you should, of course, always have an agenda. This will help you keep to the point, and will also be appreciated by the attendees, so that everybody knows what to expect. Think about the running order for the presentation. For example, should you put the contentious issues first or last?

What to expect

As part of your preparation, you should consider the potential questions and views that each attendee might have.

- Project Board
  Try and identify the overall concerns that the Project Board may have so that you can prepare and research your answers ahead of time. After all, while the project in its own right may have valuable deliverables, the Project Board will need to view the project from a wider perspective. For example:
  - How will the deliverables from this project be adopted into the company?
  - How long will this process take and what are the likely difficulties?
  - Which areas will be using the outcome and how will they be trained?
  - How will the results of this project affect other initiatives that are under way in other parts of the company?
- Executive
  - Does the project support the current corporate strategy?

- Is the Business Case acceptable?
- Are the risks manageable and acceptable?
- Do the acceptance criteria clearly reflect any stage payments to which they relate?
- Senior User
  - Have all the requirements been captured in the quality expectations?
  - Are the acceptance criteria specified to a level of detail that will enable sign-off?
- Senior Supplier
  - Is the Project Plan achievable?

REQUIRED RESOURCES

Appropriate action	Required resource	Comments
Assembling the PID	**Who?** • Project manager **What?** • All information produced and gathered during initiation	More information on the content can be found in the document maps in Appendix A.
Presenting the PID	**Who?** • Project manager • Project Board • Project Assurance • Interested parties (corporate/stakeholders) • (Team manager) **What?** • Outputs from planning software • Presentation visuals • Outside Information • Stakeholder information	When presenting the PID you might need to refer to other areas of the business. Ensure that you have all relevant information to hand. Knowing the interests and views of stakeholders is crucial to the way your presentation will be given (and received!)

Chapter 7

Stage planning

OVERVIEW

The Project Plan that was created during initiation will probably be high-level. If you have a project of a short duration (less than two to three months), then you might have planned your project in detail during initiation. If not, then you will need to plan in more detail for each stage that has been identified. Remember that stages on the Project Plan are flexible and may be moved to reflect the situation of the project.

APPROPRIATE ACTIONS
Creating the Stage Plan

Each stage of your project must be planned in detail to ensure a full understanding of activities and costs.

Chapter 4 describes the product-based planning technique. You should use this technique to help you plan the stage. Use the Project Plan to identify the high-level products that will need breaking down. You will then be able to identify the activities required to progress through the stage. Diagram 16 overleaf gives a simple indication of 'expanding' the information from project to stage level.

There are various techniques to planning. PRINCE2 assumes that you use product-based planning and a software tool for scheduling, resourcing and monitoring. Consider using a bottom-up technique for Stage Plans by obtaining team plans from the team managers, and using these to assemble the overall Stage Plan. This will ensure that the teams

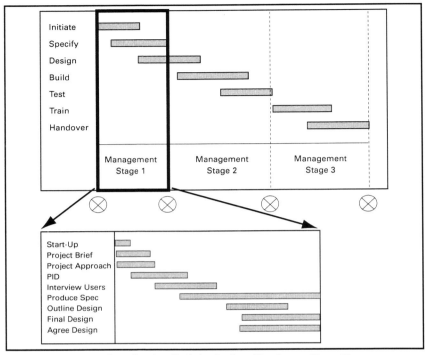

Diagram 16: Expanding the detail of the Project Plan into a Stage Plan

are involved with planning, that the Product Descriptions have been written by the right people, and it will save you from starting with a blank sheet.

The steps for planning the stage are:

- Examine the Project Plan
- Extract high-level information from the PID
  - Organisation
  - Risks
  - Product Descriptions
  - Costs
- Break down to a lower level using product-based planning technique
- Work with teams to create team plans

- Estimating effort
- Scheduling activities
- Finalise team plan
- Use team plans to assemble the Stage Plan
- Feed results back to the Project Plan
  - Review project timescales
  - Analyse project risks
- Analyse risks associated with the Stage Plan
  - How much activity is happening at once?
  - Are dependencies 'butting' together?
  - What would be the impact of late delivery?
  - What would be the impact of extra costs?
  - Re-work plan where required
- Revisit Project Plan if necessary
- Create a simple report outlining resources required
- Complete summary report
  - Assumptions made
  - Risks
  - Monitoring & control
- Create a report showing impacts to the Project Plan, Business Case and Risk Log within an End Stage Report (see Chapter 10).

A PRINCE2 plan is more that just a Gantt chart – supporting information needs to accompany the plan. When presenting the plan for approval, you should have the following information available:

- Next Stage Plan
  - Schedule (Gantt chart)
  - Activity diagram (logic network)
  - Resources report (effort & costs required)
  - Plan text (stating assumptions, risks, monitoring)
  - Relevant Product Descriptions
  - Product-based planning diagrams (where required)

- End Stage Report
  - Report on how current stage was managed
  - Confirmation that all products were completed
  - Impacts of current stage, and next Stage Plans
    - Project Plan
    - Business Case
    - Risk Log

It is essential to keep an eye on the three changeable products (Project Plan, Business Case, and Risk Log) to ensure that they still fit in with the way you have planned the stage.

Include the management activities in your Stage Plan. You will need to allocate time and resources for reporting, auditing, meetings with the Project Board and teams, examining issues and analysing risks. On top of that, you will need to motivate the teams, keep stakeholders informed, ease the anxieties of other interested parties, and re-plan where necessary.

There will always be occurrences that have not been planned. It is not always possible to place any contingency for such occurrences. This is where you will need to 'make it work' within the tolerances you negotiate with the Project Board. Tolerance is 'the permissible deviation from a plan's estimated time and cost without escalating the deviation to the next level of management'. When you have completed your plan, you will need to assess the accuracy of the estimations, and decide on the level of tolerance you will negotiate with the Project Board. The negotiation should ideally happen before the End Stage Assessment and be incorporated into the plan for approval.

Stage Quality Plan

You will also need to incorporate a stage quality plan into your Stage Plan. This should indicate more detailed requirements of the quality standards to be used during development of products and progression of the stage.

The quality review team should be identified, with statements of who will be quality reviewing which products. You should indicate on the Stage Plan when the reviews will take place and who will be involved. You need to indicate:

- when the reviews will take place
- the format for each review
  - informal
  - formal
- who will be involved
  - quality review chairperson
  - producer (team manager or team member)
  - reviewers

This information can go towards completing a Product Checklist. The Product Checklist is a list of products derived from the Product Breakdown Structure. When you have scheduled your activities, you can add the start and end dates of each product's development. When you have completed the Quality Plan, you can insert the dates of the reviews. This information will give a clear indication of when each product is being worked on.

See overleaf for REQUIRED RESOURCES.

REQUIRED RESOURCES

Appropriate action	Required resource	Comments
Stage Plan	**Who?** • Project manager • Team manager • Teams **What?** • Planning tools • Estimation tools • Project Plan	Getting the specialist teams to write the Product Descriptions will ensure that their technical skills are used for designing the solution. These will obviously be based on the requirements of the customer. The user community will sign off all Product Descriptions when they are presented at the End Stage Assessment – user and supplier working together!
Stage quality plan	**Who?** • Project manager • Quality assurance • Quality review team **What?** • QMS • Project Quality Plan • Product Descriptions	Identify the reviewers early on. Plan reviews during development, as well as at the end of development, so that faults can be acted upon earlier.

Part 3

Managing the project

Chapter 8

Getting the work done

OVERVIEW

To get any work done, an agreement and authorisation of work must exist between management and development. PRINCE2 provides the use of Work Packages to host the requirements of the work to be undertaken. The Work Package essentially acts as a 'contract' between the project manager and the team manager.

As the stage progresses and products are completed and returned to the project manager, the Stage Plan needs to be updated to reflect what has happened. This chapter explains the approaches and techniques that might help you to complete this.

APPROPRIATE ACTIONS
Work Packages

The Work Package is the formal title used by PRINCE2 to describe the information and the instructions that are collated by the project manager to enable them to pass responsibility to a team manager or team member, ie, someone who is going to take responsibility for actually doing the work.

Each package represents a very important point within the project. As you create and authorise a team to take on a Work Package, you are moving the project forward and getting product creation under way. It is also a vital mechanism for keeping control of the project, as PRINCE2 states that work should only 'commence and continue with the consent of the project manager'. To control progress of the project, work must be carried out in a logical sequence, ie, according to the plan. Authorising Work Packages enables that to happen; without this authorisation, teams cannot start work on products, even though they may be ready or have some free time available.

As the project manager it is important that, when you ask someone to carry out work on the project, you provide him or her with all the relevant information. Using the structure of a Work Package set out in PRINCE2 will help you adopt this discipline, as by following the structure you are less likely to leave out requirements, background information or details about how the work should be carried out. To maintain effective control of the project, you should maximise the time you spend managing the work. Therefore, with a Work Package you are aiming for a complete and unambiguous statement of what is to be done, so that the team can get on and do the work without constantly referring to you, with all the delays and hold-ups that this can cause.

This chapter assumes that the Work Package will be handled formally; therefore the Work Package will be a document which is written up and can be signed off between you and your team manager. However, if preferred, the Work Package can be a verbal instruction between you and your team manager. Whether you take a formal or an informal work approach depends on the following factors:

- Complexity of the work – if there are many special instructions and detailed information to be passed across, a written record would be more appropriate.
- Previous experience of the work – if the work is simple, straightforward, well understood (perhaps it is a regular and frequently carried out piece of work) and relatively short term, then a verbal Work Package may be more suitable.
- Status of the team manager – if the team manager and/or their team work for an external organisation, then a written record would be best.

The main contents of a Work Package are:

- Product Description
  - A Copy of each of the Product Descriptions needed to develop the Products within this piece of work (See Chapter 4 for details of Product Descriptions)
- Techniques/Processes/Procedures to be used
  - As required by the Customer Organisation and Project Board
- Interfaces
  - Relationships with other projects, programmes and existing facilities
- Stage Plan Extract
  - A statement of the key dates extracted from the management Stage Plan
- Constraints: Time/Cost/Tolerance/Interfaces
  - To be inserted following discussion and agreement between the project manager and team manager
- Reporting
  - The format, content and frequency of Checkpoint Reports (and any other form of reporting required).
- Product Handover Requirements
  - Stating the return arrangements and how notification is to be made
- Quality checking requirements
  - Agreed arrangements for carrying out quality reviews, Inspections, Tests etc. Format for the Quality Log to be maintained for the Product(s)

Why create a formal Work Package? It:
- helps avoid misunderstandings
- provides a link to performance assessment
- can allow for extra information to be set out in the contract
- there is less chance things will be missed or forgotten

- gives the team manager a document to review and clarify before starting work
- avoids reliance on memories of a conversation between the project manager and the team manager
- saves the team manager having to document work for the team members
- adds to a more focused discussion between the project manager and the team manager on whether there are enough resources to carry out the work as
  (a) they can walk through Product Descriptions and other parts of Work Package and point out concerns
  (b) the team manager can draw up a team plan which highlights where resources are short.

The main benefit to you is that you will find out at the beginning if the deadlines set for the work were over-ambitious or if your budget calculations were under-estimated. Even if the Work Package was drafted with the relevant team manager, it does not hurt to go through a formal acceptance of the work; it will act as a double-check on everything that was written and agreed. Without this formality at the start of the work, these issues will be reported during the work where it is more difficult to stand back from them and come up with contingency plans and alternative arrangements.

A formal structure gives you an opportunity to pass on other more 'informal' concerns regarding, for example:

- areas of particular interest from other departments or members of the Project Board
- auditing or regulatory issues which the team manager needs to be aware of

Highlight any key interim deliverables and milestone dates (which might be based around other issues on the project, eg, user group meetings, company strategic reviews, audits etc). Discuss with the team manager how checkpoints should be tied to these dates.

All contractors (prime and sub) can be reviewed using the following quality criteria for the Work Package:

- Is the required Work Package clearly defined and understood by the assigned resource?
- Is there a Product Description for the required products with clearly identified and acceptable quality criteria?
- Does the Product Description match up with the other Work Package documentation?
- Are standards for the work agreed?
- Are the defined standards in line with those applied to similar products?
- Have all necessary interfaces been defined?
- Do the reporting arrangements include the provision for Exception Reporting?
- Is there agreement between the project manager and recipient on exactly what is to be done?
- Is there agreement on the constraints, including effort, cost and targets?
- Are the dates and effort in line with those shown in the Stage Plan?
- Are reporting arrangements defined?
- Is any requirement for independent attendance at, and participation in, quality checking defined?

Interfaces/interdependencies

When there are several people or teams at work developing products, it is important to understand the complex interdependencies. It is not as simple as saying A must be finished before B and B must be finished before C. Does all of A need to be completed before B can start?

While the process of authorising a Work Package has many benefits, it is important to ensure that the level to which it is applied is appropriate, otherwise it can be seen as very bureaucratic and can be reducing motivation for the teams involved. For a piece of work which will take only a few days to complete, and is something of which the team manager and team members have experience, you should not pull together a 60-page dossier, with every minute detail, process and technique specified. Stating the obvious can be seen as not trusting the team to work things out for themselves, or insulting their intelligence.

Once you have gathered all the information, it needs to be passed to the team manager or the team member responsible. In order to ensure that there are no misunderstandings, PRINCE2 has a process that specifically covers this handover. It is called accepting a Work Package, and its fundamental principle is that there should be agreement between the project manager and the team manager on:

- What is to be delivered
- What constraints apply
- Any interfaces to be recognised
- Whether the requirements of the Work Package are reasonable and can be achieved.

This agreement can take many forms. There may be a meeting, or telephone call between you; or it may be done remotely by sending the Work Package and awaiting comments. This form of the agreement will be guided by factors such as:

- The involvement that the team manager had in creating the Work Package
- The complexity of the work
- The relationship between the project manager and the team manager
- The amount of experience that the project manager and team manager have of the work
- The risks associated with the work

Involvement of team managers in creating Work Packages

Even though it is the responsibility of the project manager to collate the information for the Work Package, the team manager may have had some involvement. This is especially true if it is a very specialist piece of work, for which the team manager has expertise. In this case, the project manager can work in conjunction with the team manager to participate in writing the Product Description, techniques to be used and type of quality checks to be carried out. Also the project manager can specify any constraints or interfaces based on a wider knowledge of the project and the reporting requirements, amount of time available, etc, based on the project manager's need to control the project.

Complexity

If the work is of a complex and/or specialist nature, the team manager may be an appropriate resource on which to call when pulling together the Work Package. If interfaces between this work and other work on the project are to be maintained during product creation, then involvement of other team managers from the project in drafting the Work Package might be helpful.

Relationships

If you have not worked previously together, it can be a good idea to hold a meeting to discuss the Work Package. It will give you a chance to get to know each other a little better. Throughout the work, the team manager will be an important part of the project so it is important to have a good working relationship. You can get to know how each of you likes to work – even simple things like how much detail you like to see in the Checkpoint Reports or the best time to send in reports, etc, will show you.

Experience and expertise

If you have a great deal of experience in the work, you might want to arrange a meeting so that, in addition to all of the details set out in the

Work Package, you can pass on some of your knowledge, or informally let the team manager know that you are available as a reference point if he/she runs into difficulties. Alternatively, if the team manager is an expert, it can be useful to meet to develop your own understanding of the work. This could include getting the team manager to point out any particularly difficult or straightforward aspects of the work to give advanced warning of areas that might not go as smoothly as the plan indicates. After all, no one expects you to have as much detailed knowledge of the work as the experts you have employed to do it. However, as it is often you, and not the team manager who will have to 'walk' the Project Board through progress and issues, any knowledge and understanding you can gain will be very helpful.

Risks

All projects have an element of risk. This increases if, for example:

- The work is new territory for either you, or even for the organisation that has commissioned the project
- It is very specialist and therefore it has been difficult to state all of the requirements, as these are still evolving.

The team manager must bring specialist knowledge of the work to bear, to ensure that any risks associated with the Work Package are acknowledged, relevant actions identified, planned and resourced. While the project manager has been responsible for the overall identification of risks throughout the project, the team manager may well be able to identify further risks based on deeper understanding of the work. These risks can relate to either problems associated with the actual development of the products, or can be potential problems that the users might face when the products go into operation.

Team Plans

In order for the team manager to confirm that the requirements of the

Work Package are reasonable, and that it can be completed within the time frame, budget and other constraints, a team plan may be produced, or the existing team plan updated.

Team plans are created using exactly the same planning methodology described for creation of the Stage Plans. This should be done before work starts, so that both the project manager and the team manager have a degree of confidence that there are sufficient resources available, with the right level of skills.

Accepting and agreeing how the work will be completed

If there are any doubts about whether or not the Work Package can actually be completed on time or to budget, it is best to know up front so that the work can be split across several Work Packages if necessary. Other teams can then become involved to shoulder the workload. One specific area that the team manager should look for is that sufficient budget and time have been allocated to carry out the quality checking of the products created. It is one of the areas most easily overlooked, as emphasis naturally is always given to the actual creation of the products.

The process of accepting a Work Package may involve a degree of negotiation by both parties, to ensure that what is being asked can actually be achieved. The team manager may ask you to find more resources, or provide him/her with more time, money or materials in order to get the job done. The Work Package may also include work which they feel is better done by others in the project; you may be called on to adjust your Stage and Project Plan if that turns out to be the case. At the end of accepting the Work Package, the team manager must ensure that there is full understanding of what is required, so that work can commence.

This acceptance process is important to both parties. It is an opportunity for the team manager to take part in the management of the work, which is important for motivation and team building. For the team manager, it provides a formal structure through which his or her expertise and technical knowledge can be used to shape the work that is being done, but within the structure of a specific piece of work. You must retain overall responsibility for authorising work, but that does not mean that advice, guidance and input from the team managers should not be sought.

In addition to ensuring that the work can be created within the constraints, the team manager must confirm the completion and handover procedures.

Understand how and from whom approval for the products is to be obtained

On completion of the Work Package, the ultimate recipients of the products may be involved in their approval. This approval should be done before the project manager is notified that the product is complete, and can perhaps be carried out at a lower level than the ultimate acceptance which comes from the Project Board at the End Stage Assessment.

Understand how the approved products are to be formally handed over

What is the configuration management method in use on the project and is it clearly understood? From a practical perspective, this might mean knowing how version numbers are to be assigned, and the naming conventions that are in use (See Chapters 3 & 5).

Also, at a lower level, how will products be controlled across the team? The team members need to know these processes, so that the completed work is controlled by the team manager, and not handed over to recipients in an informal manner.

Confirm how the project manager is to be informed of completion of the Work Package

It is vital that, as products are completed (including each successful quality review), the project manager is informed. If there is a specific way that you are to be notified of completions, either in writing or verbally, then the team manager must be informed, and you must make it clear whether Project Support should also be alerted so that the configuration records can be updated.

Once the Work Package has been accepted, the full responsibility of managing the development of the products stated therein and reporting on any progress to the project manager rests with the team manager. In PRINCE2 terminology, we are now dealing with 'Execution of the Work Package'.

There are two parts to the development of the products and the team manager is responsible for both.

Carrying out the work

We obviously cannot go into any detail on the creation of specific products but we can discuss some of the management techniques that the team manager needs to apply during project creation.

Monitoring and controlling the risks associated with the Work Package

The team manager should identify potential risks with the work when accepting a Work Package. During the creation of the products, any actions required to mitigate these risks should be implemented. Once implemented, the team manager should check that the action is having the desired effect and, if not, step in and identify further actions that should be carried out.

Monitoring and controlling problems that arise during product creation

The team manager should advise the project manager of any problems that might affect the agreed tolerance for the Work Package via a Project Issue. As part of the Work Package, it needs to be made clear to the team manager what the arrangements for change control are on this project. This is especially true if the team manager is from an external supplier.

Quality checking of the products

Quality checking of the products determines if they are complete, that is, that they match the description detailed in the Product Description, and that they fulfil all the quality criteria, also detailed in the Product Description. A finished Work Package must have products that are 'fit for purpose'. Reporting that a Work Package is finished, when products do not meet this criteria, is actually reporting false progress. The team manager retains responsibility for the work until it is completely right; the only exception is when a problem arises which prevents completion, and the issue is then escalated to the project manager.

Products are checked for completion using the PRINCE2 quality reviews. This emphasises the actual assessment and sign-off of the product; it doesn't provide a forum for discussing ways to correct or improve the product. Therefore, the review should be a straightforward analytical process of comparing the product to the Product Description, rather than a session of emotional arguments of what is correct, or blame if things are incorrect.

The people participating in the reviews should have a vested interest in achieving completion of the product, and in ensuring that it is correct. These two interests are not always the same (or aligned). The producer of the product and the supplier (perhaps both from the same organisation) will have a vested interest in completion of the product, especially if completion is tied to payment. Those from the customer will have a vested interest in ensuring the product is complete because they will be either using the product, or will be relying on its results. They also have a vested interest in seeing its completion, as obviously they will be keen to move the project forward, and deliver on time.

To balance these potentially conflicting interests it is vital to include Project Assurance, if not in the actual reviews then at least in planning the reviews and checking that they have actually taken place correctly. The Project Assurance people will be able to advise on suitable reviewers for each review based on their knowledge of the overall project outcome (which gives them a good all-round perspective) as well as their understanding of the progress that has been made in the checking process so far. It is helpful sometimes to be able to state that this 'independent' advice has been sought, particularly if the review produces contentious findings. An example of this is when you have to deal with an aggrieved team manager or team member who feels that their work has been picked apart unnecessarily harshly.

Project Assurance can also be used as a resource to train participants in the technique of quality reviews; making sure everyone is aware of their role and responsibilities; and that they are properly briefed before carrying out the reviews.

One of the key aspects to address is the need for the reviewers to approach the review with the right perspective. They are looking for defects in the products, not in the work of the producer. Therefore, the review must in no way become a witch-hunt. All those participating in the review should adopt a 'team' attitude, where the team has a common goal to identify if the product is correct and, if not, to identify rework.

It may seem obvious but reviewers should actually carry out the review before the review meeting. Everyone has busy schedules and there is always a temptation to believe that a review can be left to the last minute, or can actually be carried out while other colleagues are presenting their findings. This is a waste of time, and risks errors not being picked up.

The review meetings must be organised, chaired and concluded with a recommendation of either acceptance or rework. The Review Chairperson performs this role. In order to ensure the smooth running of the meeting, this person must have a balance between the two interests detailed above. We would argue that his or her knowledge of the product does not need to be extensive. It is the ability to chair meetings successfully which is vital. The key qualities and skills required are:

- ability to listen
- skill in encouraging participation

- skill in maintaining momentum of discussion
- an ability to make an unbiased contribution
- skill in concluding and summarising the meeting

The type of review is very much dependent on the type of product. If it is a document then reading it and checking its content, format, grammar, style, length, etc, should be sufficient. For other products, demonstrations, walk-throughs, trial runs or visual inspections might be more appropriate. Whatever type of check is carried out, the reviewer's understanding of the quality criteria, and especially the priority is important. Emphasis is on ensuring the product is 'fit for purpose' but, at the same time, a level of pragmatism is needed if the process is not to grind to a halt when minor errors are discovered. Before recommending re-work, the reviewer must balance the need to correct the error against the cost, time and knock-on effects of carrying out the correction.

Reviewers should be provided with a question list, which sets out each of the quality criteria, with a checkbox to indicate if the criteria have been met or not. There should be space on this question list for the reviewer to note any errors. If it is more practical, errors can be annotated directly onto the product where they are written products, or drawings or designs.

Before the review meeting the completed question lists and the copies of the products (especially if they have been annotated with errors) should be returned to the producer. The Review Chairperson should gather the lists from each of the reviewers. The aim is not to spring product complaints onto the producer at the review meeting. Reviewers should be interested in ensuring that the producer knows exactly what they have found wrong with the products so that they can be put right.

The three main aims of the review meeting are to discuss, clarify and reach agreement on the points raised by the reviewers and the outcome of the review. There are three possible outcomes to the review meeting:

- Sign-off of the product as complete
  - The product can be signed-off immediately, and notification of this passed onto the project manager and team manager
- Errors are identified but the product can be signed-off
  - Once the errors have been corrected the product can be signed off as completed without a further quality review having to take place.
- Errors are identified that will radically alter the product
  - The errors that have been found cannot be corrected with some simple rework. In putting the errors right, there will be a significant change to the product, which means that the review process should start all over again.

After the meeting, these follow-up actions should be carried out. The project manager or team manager is notified of the result and sign-off is completed or a plan of remedial work is created.

If the results of the review meeting cannot be agreed, then this in itself should be raised as a follow-on item and the project manager alerted. Some type of action will have to be taken, as the Work Package cannot be left in limbo.

If the problem affects products other than just that being reviewed, then it should be raised via a Project Issue.

A guiding principle of quality reviews is that they must concentrate on the status of the product, and not turn into a forum for finding solutions to the errors. If errors exist then in the first case it is the responsibility of the producer and their team (if applicable) to find ways to fix the problems. The people gathered together for a review are not necessarily the right people to identify how to fix things. They will not necessarily have all the relevant technical skills. Also, if the review becomes a forum for solving problems, it will not be able to keep to the schedule set out in the Stage Plan. Finding solutions should be undertaken with the right people, with the right amount of time to solve them, and this does not belong in a review meeting.

This chapter has looked at the quality review technique from the perspective of the larger project but it can be scaled to suit the size of the project, the number of people involved in development, etc. After all, a team of reviewers and a Review Chairperson is simply not practical for a project team of two team members and a project manager. In this case a simple check by one person, and a follow-up meeting with the producer is sufficient.

Once the product has successfully passed its product review, it must be handed over by the team manager. Products may be handed back directly to the project manager, or they go via the Configuration Librarian. If a number of products are to be created as the result of one Work Package, then it may be agreed that these products are submitted to the configuration librarian individually, and the project manager is only informed when all products constituting the whole Work Package have been completed.

Handover takes place once acceptance of the products has been received from the recipients and the Configuration Librarian. The recipients are representatives from the users, who will ultimately have to use the products or will depend on the results of the product.

The team manager also has to check that the Quality Log entries are up to date and complete, and that any statistics that relate to the product are passed to the project manager. For example, actual effort, cost, time, etc, compared to their estimates is useful information that should be recorded in the Stage Plan. This can then be used to review estimates of other work yet to be done, to see if these estimates need to be altered in light of the most recent experience.

At this time the team manager may also pass on any incidents that should be added to the Lessons Learned Log. The project manager is responsible for maintaining this log, but obviously it should include experiences from all members of the project organisation.

While PRINCE2 provides a framework for the day-to-day management of the project, there is no similar information set out for the day-to-day management of the work. However, the principles remain the same. Throughout the creation and quality checking of the products, the team manager must undertake this day-to-day management. This will include assessing and reporting on the progress of development, issues, risks and quality checking.

Capture and management of the work

PRINCE2 stresses that, throughout the work, it is important that the team manager keeps an up-to-date record of the amount of effort the work is taking. In this case, effort means the amount of time, money and other resources used. There are many obvious reasons why this information is important, but it is worth having a look at some of the key reasons:

Assessing progress

Up-to-date progress information is crucial and you must ensure that whatever information is required is understood by both the producer of the work and the team manager. Otherwise, when the team manager requests information that the producer has not been tracking, or does not have a record of, time will be wasted by the producer collecting this information. Agreement should be reached on some of the following questions:

- Should records be kept in hours or days? Depending on the sophistication of the organisation, time recording and other systems may be in place which will assist in collecting this data.
- Does each team member need to keep a record of his /her individual effort?
- What materials costs need to be included?

Integrity of estimating

If the effort actually being used differs significantly from that planned, then estimates may need to be revised for other areas of work. It is better to know this as far in advance as possible, so that these revised estimates can be created, and any knock-on effects to these changes can also be dealt with.

Work Package status

The status of the Work Package relates to the overall work that is being undertaken, rather than any specific products that are being created. Therefore, some examples of the different types of status will include:

- In progress and on time
- In progress but late
- In progress and ahead of schedule
- Delayed start
- Completed on time
- Completed late
- Completed ahead of schedule
- In progress and on budget
- In progress but over budget
- In progress and under budget
- Completed and on budget
- Completed but over budget
- Completed and under budget

To ensure that the details of this reporting do not become overly complicated or take too long to create, the project can apply a traffic light system of reporting, ie, Red, Amber or Green. This is an effective way of grading problems with the Work Package, and can quickly draw attention to areas requiring further action.

The seriousness of budget and schedule overruns can be graded and agreed by all members of the project management team before work starts. For example:

- Red – more than 10% over budget or over schedule
- Amber – between 5% and 10% over budget or over schedule
- Green – no more than 5% over budget or over schedule

Without the recording of actual effort, it will not be possible to identify if the Work Package is likely to exceed the tolerance allowed. So the sooner the tolerance is identified as being exceeded, the earlier the issue can be escalated for corrective action and there are likely to be more options for correcting the problem.

Determine the status of each product

It is important to agree across the project team the possible different types of status that a product can have and what each status type means. For example:

1. Planned – the existence of the product is known, a Work Package has been created, but has not yet been started.
2. Work in progress – the Work Package for the product has been started
3. Under review – initial creation of the product has been completed and the quality review process has begun
4. Re-work – the product did not pass its quality review, and re-work is being started, before returning to a status of under review.
5. Completed – the product has successfully completed its quality review and has been recorded in the configuration item record as completed.

Report on risks to project manager

When agreeing a Work Package, the team manager may have pointed out specialist risks associated with the work. When the products are being created, the status of these risks should be monitored, so that if action is required it is carried out promptly. The project manager, as holder of the Risk Log, should be kept informed of any changes to the status of existing risks, the identification of new risks and any actions taken to deal with them.

Evaluate with the producer the amount of effort still required

When work is allocated to individuals, it is important to ensure that they understand what is being asked of them, how much time, money and other resources are to be used, and that the necessary deadlines for the work are understood. At this point, this information is based upon estimates, so the producer should be recognised as a valuable source of up-to-date information, which can be fed back into the estimating process.

Feed progress back to project manager

It is essential that the project manager is kept up to date with the progress of the Work Package. However, the team manager should guard against deluging the project manager with information that is really only relevant to the team. The key information required is:

- The status of the products associated with the Work Package
- Percentage complete of the Work Package
- Problems identified and actions taken to resolve them, if the problem and solution could have an impact on other products outside of the Work Package. In this way, the project manager can pass on helpful experience to others working on the project.

REQUIRED RESOURCES

Appropriate action	Required resource	Comments
Work Package	**Who?** • Project manager • Team manager • Purchasing and/or procurement staff **What?** • Stage Plan • Team plans • Contract information	Careful thought needs to be applied when creating the Work Package so that purchasing 'rights' are recognised between yourself, the customer and supplier. Formal contracts with external suppliers in particular will need to be drawn up carefully. This could be a task assigned to a procurement division (using a Work Package!)
Assessing progress	**Who?** • Project manager • Team manager • Project support • Project assurance **What?** • Stage Plan • Checkpoint Reports • Issue Log • Quality Log • Daily Log	As products are returned to configuration management, project support can update the Stage Plan for the project manager. Project Assurance should ensure that the updates reflect the current situation. Ad hoc advice and information from external sources might need to be represented on the plan. Any events that have resulted in slippages to specialist work, or management work, should also be updated in the plan.

Chapter 9

Reporting

OVERVIEW

This chapter explains the two time-driven reports of a PRINCE2 project: the Highlight Report and the Checkpoint Report. The Highlight Report is a progress summary from the project manager to the Project Board, and the Checkpoint Report is a report from the team manager to the project manager.

Reporting progress is the key information flow throughout the life of the project. The Project Board must be kept informed regularly of work that is effectively done in their name. They do not work on the project full time; the Highlight Reports are their lifeline to the project.

As project manager you will be unable to provide them with relevant information if you are not kept informed of the detailed work. The Checkpoint Reports are your lifeline.

APPROPRIATE ACTIONS

While the structure of both reports is similar, they are for two very different audiences, so we have covered them separately, below.

Highlight Report

The Highlight Report is the main means of communication between the project manager and the Project Board. The key to creating management confidence is good reporting and a clear information flow. The purpose of the report is to allow the Project Board to 'manage by exception'.

The Highlight Report will confirm progress being made along the Stage Plan that the Project Board have approved. Anything outside of tolerance should be reported separately.

The report content must be kept high level and focused:

- Keep it concise
- Keep it factual
- Consider the issues most relevant to each Project Board member and ensure they are covered
- Anticipate questions from the Project Board and make sure they are answered.

Keep it concise

The Highlight Report needs to be short and to the point. If it is too long the Project Board only skim, perhaps missing vital information. Also project managers do not want to spend too much time writing long reports, when they should concentrate on the day-to-day issues of the project.

Keep it factual

The key things to avoid in a Highlight Report are guesswork and emotion. For any information provided, make sure that there is supporting information, in case they want to follow up later. The report should cover factual aspects, rather than emotional issues such as excuses, passing of blame for late running items etc. While it is cathartic to explain the reasons behind a problem so that the project is painted in the best light, it is not actually moving the project forward, so provides just a straightforward, factual account!

Consider the issues most relevant to each member and ensure they are covered

Review the structure and make-up of the Project Board, so that the Highlight Report addresses the key items of interest to those reading it.

Anticipate their questions and make sure they are answered

- The Senior User represents future users of the project's deliverables; he or she is always going to be most interested in delivery dates:
  - When will the products be ready for use?
  - When will the products be ready for testing?
  - When will training begin?
- As the Executive owns the Business Case, it is likely that he/she will have particular interest in seeing:
  - a summary of costs to date,
  - any changes in resource costs and their explanation
  - estimates of likely overall cost.
- The Senior Supplier will want to know:
  - When will specialist resources be required for the project?
  - When can they be freed up to undertake other work?

As each member of the Project Board has different interests, you may have to write a generic report. But be prepared to meet individually to go over their interest areas in more detail, eg, attend user group meetings; meet with the Executive to review the budget in detail; meet with the Senior Supplier to review technical aspects in detail. You will have to make a decision on whether this is a worthwhile use of your time, or whether it is divisive. It may have risks in discussing aspects of the project individually with Project Board members, rather than keeping them all up to speed with all areas of the project.

If you are concerned by an apparent lack of commitment from any member of the Project Board, the Highlight Report can be a subtle tool in alerting other members to your concerns. The report can detail areas where there has been a lack of co-operation or progress and, when this is contrasted with areas where progress is good, it can alert the other board members to your concern. After all, it is more effective if the Executive applies pressure to this lack of commitment, as it carries the most weight managerially. However, this action should only be considered once the problem has been brought to the attention of the Project Board member concerned. Don't complain about lack of action in the Highlight Report until you have brought it to their attention and still failed to get action. Alert them to the problems via a meeting or phone call and work with them to solve the problem. Mention this in the Highlight Report and be factual in terms of:

- the impact it is having
- any delays it is causing
- the impact of these delays on other products
- the impact of delays on morale or motivation.

For example, if a problem is resolved within a few days, how quickly will the overall project get back on its feet? This is also an opportunity to discuss how quickly the situation can be recovered and therefore potentially showing the project, and the management of the project in a positive light.

By identifying and planning the structure of reports it is possible to schedule the effort for report creation into the plans. This will reduce the likelihood that they are viewed as something that can be run off in half an hour.

Do not list all the things that are going to plan, only concentrate on things that have gone better than expected and worse than expected and things that need to be clarified.

The downside to this type of reporting is that it concentrates only on the problem areas. So, it is excellent for focusing attention on areas where decisions need to be made, but it is no use at all when the project manager is trying to maintain enthusiasm and motivation.

Checkpoint Report

This is your source of information from your team managers; you must decide exactly what you will need to know – and make sure it is included in the Checkpoint Report. Do not blame the teams for not telling you things if you have not asked for them.

The Checkpoint Report is not set in stone. Ensure that team members realise that the structure of the report will evolve as the work progresses.

Having chosen measures upon which you want to report in your Highlight Report (or in the End Stage Report or in the End Project Report) make sure that they are tracked and reported upon. Metrics can include:

- actual hours of work
- delays and who is causing them

The structure of the Checkpoint Report can be used as an agenda for the team manager to hold checkpoint meetings. It is a good idea to get the team manager involved in designing the Checkpoint Report. If it is felt to be too bureaucratic there will be a reluctance to complete it and it may build resentment. On larger projects, where several teams may be operating at once, it is easier to spot issues and trends across the project if all the Checkpoint Reports follow the same structure. It also means that no single team manager will feel that he or she is being treated any differently to anyone else. This structured approach to checkpoint or progress meetings (within the team) helps members take them seriously and prepare for them.

See overleaf for REQUIRED RESOURCES.

REQUIRED RESOURCES

Appropriate action	Required resource	Comments
Highlight Report	**Who?** • Project manager • Project Board • Project Assurance **What?** • Checkpoint Reports • Quality Log • Issue Log • Risk Log • Business Case • PID	Discussions with the Project Board members will be required to establish the format of the reports and the information the reports will contain. Other recipients of highlight reports should be documented in the Communication Plan. Other requests for copies should be cleared first with the Project Board.
Checkpoint Report	**Who?** • Team manager • Team members • Quality review team **What?** • Minutes from checkpoint meetings • Team plan • Quality Log • Work Package	Teams will be meeting on a regular basis, and the minutes from these meetings will provide the information to the project manager in the Checkpoint Reports. Details of work completed, along with forecasts for future work should be included. Information from the quality review team might be useful for details of the quality checks.

Chapter 10

When things go wrong

OVERVIEW

Within any project, changes to the scope or the specification of the products will arise, and unless they are handled in a structured way, they can easily disrupt the project schedule and divert attention away from product delivery. There will also be questions or concerns, time slippages and resource problems. All of these examples are Project Issues that need to be dealt with in a controlled manner.

APPROPRIATE ACTIONS

Project Issues can be regarded as anything that happens on the project that has not already been included in the plans.

Issues and Requests for Change can be raised by anyone, whether they are part of the project team or not, and they can be raised at any time. In this chapter, we set out an approach for dealing with these 'interruptions' so that you can still get on with managing the project.

PRINCE2 suggests a structure for carefully controlling issues and changes. The key steps required to adopt this structure are:

- capturing Project Issues
- examining Project Issues
- reviewing stage status
- taking corrective action
- escalating issues

Capturing Project Issues

However insignificant the issue may appear, it must be recorded and its receipt acknowledged. This ensures that nothing gets overlooked. It is especially important for items that initially look fairly harmless but turn out to be much bigger to deal with than first thought. If you let the originator know that you are dealing with it, you will avoid those annoying phone calls and emails – 'I've sent you an issue. Did you receive it, are you dealing with it yet?' – that always arrive when you are at your busiest.

In PRINCE2, issues are recorded in the Issues Log. This provides a record of the analysis and status of the issue. There is one Issue Log for the whole project and it is the responsibility of the project manager to ensure all issues are recorded in it. This activity can be delegated to the Configuration Librarian if one has been appointed, although it is still vital that the project manager reviews the Issue Log regularly, especially to check the progress of all 'open' items.

When an issue is recorded in the Issue Log it should be allocated a unique reference number and the issue should be assigned a category. It is useful to categorise issues according to type. This will make reporting on issues easier, as you can search the issues log by category.

PRINCE2 suggests that the categories should be:

● Request for change
● Off-specification
● General issue

However, for large and complex projects, where the number of issues is expected to be high, it is a good idea to categorise the issues into groupings that can be tracked more easily than the general categories shown above.

These other categorisations might include:

● Change in requirements
  • User-driven change (having seen the product, users may suggest

changes based on the way in which the product will be used in the workplace)

- Technical reason for change (eg, original scope not technically possible)

● Change in environment
  - Legislative change
  - Strategic change/change in direction by the company
  - New customer
  - New supplier
  - Unexpected change to project management team
  - Actions by a competitor
  - Programme management directive
  - Reorganisation of the company
  - Problem not previously identified during risk analysis
  - Problem previously identified during risk analysis
  - Error in completed work
  - Error in work in progress

Agreeing these categories in advance of the project getting under way will assist in your analysis as you are more likely to be comparing like for like.

Look for trends

When each issue is considered individually, it is sometimes difficult to see a pattern, which might be indicating a more serious problem. For example, frequent changes to products might mean that thorough identification of product requirements and customers quality expectations was not carried out at the start of the project, leading to this constant 'fire fighting' once the project is under way.

Another risk arising from the individual assessment of issues is that it hides their cumulative effect on the stage overall. By recording each issue in the Issue Log, it is easier to see just how many issues are being raised, how frequently, and if there is any pattern or trend.

What does the change affect?

PRINCE2 suggests that a distinction is made between changes that affect something that has already been completed and approved, and something that either has not yet been worked on or is work in progress.

If the change relates to a product that has already been approved by the Project Board and is deemed as complete, then it cannot be changed unless the Board give their approval to the change.

If the product is still under construction, then it may be possible to incorporate the change into the existing work. However, before undertaking any work, it is worth considering whether the issue can be fixed within stage tolerances. Also, it is helpful to find out if the Senior User thinks it is worthwhile making the change.

Impact of change

Prior to starting any work to fix the issue, it is very important that the full scale of the work involved is understood. This includes looking at the full impact of the change, including its knock-on effects.

Examining Project Issues

Each issue must be examined against a set of criteria and make sure you have information on all of them; don't leap to a conclusion based on limited information. For example, if something looks like it is just a cosmetic change, you might try and save time by just looking at how long it will take to make the change (i.e, the impact on the schedule). But by ignoring all other factors or criteria, you might miss gathering some vital information, eg, that the cosmetic change has a knock-on effect to the Business Case; the product will no longer be acceptable in certain markets and therefore, cannot generate all of the envisaged in the Business Case.

PRINCE2 suggests that all available and relevant information is gathered about the issue. Use this information to examine the effect of the issue on the following factors:

- Stage cost
- Stage timescale
- Project cost
- Project timescale
- Ability to achieve benefits (examine each benefit separately to see if it has no effect, not applicable or has effect)
- Risks
- Project purpose
- Customer's quality expectations

To expedite the analysis of Project Issues, PRINCE2 suggests that the person who originates the issue also identifies how serious they believe it to be. The categories suggested in PRINCE2 are shown below:

- Must – the final product will not work, or will not meet quality standards without this change.
- Important change – use of the final product will require a work-around without this change.
- Nice to have – by implementing this change, the customer would find the product easier to use, or would enjoy the product more in some way.
- Cosmetic change – of no importance to a product, e.g, change of colour or layout, formatting changes; does not change any working part of the product.
- No change – a question or query.

Reviewing stage status

When the Project Issue is understood in more detail, it is a good idea to review the current Stage Plan for two pieces of information:

- How serious in terms of impact on the stage is the issue?
  - Is it halting progress on the current Work Package?
  - Is it having any knock-on effects for other Work Packages?

- What impact will handling the issue have on the Stage Plan?
  - In terms of the length of the overall stage, what is the impact of each option?
  - Are there any knock-on effects to other related Work Packages?

Re-planning

During the course of any stage, there will often be a need to carry out re-planning of some sort. When Project Issues are raised, they will need to be examined and it will need to be determined whether the tolerance that has been authorised has been exceeded. A structured approach to this is:

- What is the problem?
- What can be done about it?
- Is the budget available to deal with it?
- Is there time available to deal with it?
- Are other resources available to carry out the work?

The project manager will need to speak to the users and suppliers to understand the impact of most issues. Where the issue can be addressed within the constraints, the changes will still need to be represented on the Stage Plan. There will no doubt be additional activity, or maybe time added to the work. The planning principles outlined earlier in this book should be used for this corrective planning. It might be possible to use cost tolerance to pay for overtime which will help to bring the stage back into target.

As well as updating the Stage Plan, changes to any Work Packages that need be updated should be issued and Work Packages created if necessary. The latter should go through the normal authorising Work Packages routine.

Where the impact of a Project Issue is forecast to drive the stage outside tolerance, an Exception Report can be used to escalate the problem (see above). Further action will then be triggered by one of several responses:

- Keep going in the current direction but ensure that the Project Board are kept informed of any change in status – however small

This might involve the Project Board increasing the tolerance of the stage in order to have the stage completed with the minimum disruption. This is usually an option towards the end of a stage or when the deviation is slight.

- Request an Exception Plan detailing the activities from the current moment to the end of the stage.

The process for creating the Exception Plan is the same as for creating the Stage Plan. However, it is important to take stock of the situation and plan from the point the project has currently reached. This almost amounts to 're-baselining' the stage so far. It is important to understand what has been achieved to date during the stage, what needs to be achieved, and how it will be done.

Possible ways of recovering the situation might include:

- Calling an end of stage with immediate effect
- Slipping products/activities to the next stage
- Drop products altogether
- Increasing budget to complete stage in time
- Increasing time to complete stage in budget
- Push the end of stage boundary back
- Terminate the project

Whatever the plan, the project manager must ensure that the Project Plan is updated accordingly. The management stages that have previously been identified as key decision points might have moved. The project itself might have become a higher risk and shorter management stages will be necessary.

As a result of all this information, the project manager should analyse all planned work for impacts on the Project Plan, Business Case and Risk Log. All this information should be presented to the Project Board who can give direction to ad hoc planning, and authorise any Exception Plans.

Taking corrective action

Examine the issue, and then make decisions about the most appropriate actions required to handle it. If you are confident that you can take these actions without having to seek approval of the Project Board, then it is important to get the work under way. A new Work Package should be created, this time specifying all actions that must be undertaken to fix the issue.

Escalating problems

If it isn't possible to fix the problem under your own management authority, then the issue will need to be raised with the Project Board. PRINCE2 recommends that you use an Exception Report to do this.

The Exception Report should not take long to write. It should be to the point, outlining the issue and the options for handling it. Remember that you are trying to communicate facts; provide enough information to the Project Board to allow them to make a decision. You may already be very familiar with all aspects but the Project Board members may need additional need some background information to allow them to see it in context.

To speed up the process of alerting the board it is useful to have a pre-prepared framework for reporting options:

- Context:
  - Even with previous regular progress reports it is still a good idea to provide some 'background' information to bring the Project Board up to speed on how the issue occurred. You could also tell them how you collected data for this report, who you spoke too, and on what basis you have made any assumptions or estimates. This

information will enable the Project Board to feel comfortable with the research you have undertaken, so that they can concentrate on evaluating the options.

- Time required to prepare implementation of the option:
  - If the options presented in the Exception Report are very high level, and a lot of research and planning is required before action can be taken, explain this. It is particularly important where the issue will lead the project into new areas of work, where there may be a learning curve for members of the project team.
- Time to carry out the option:
  - Provide an estimate of the amount of time required to manage the issue. If the actions related to the issue can be carried out alongside other tasks, state this. Otherwise, outline how the stage, and potentially the project will be delayed by dealing with this issue.
- Cost of the option:
  - The cost should be identified in terms of the amount of money required, the proportion of the project budget that this represents, the proportion of the stage budget that this represents and your recommendations for where this money can come from. Are you requesting an absolute budget increase, are you suggesting that the money is made available from the change budget (if one exists) or are you recommending that the money can be found from cost savings elsewhere in the project?
- What steps to take:
  - Include explicit steps to resolve an issue and any knock-on effects for other work in progress or future work. This includes:
    - Notifications to suppliers of changed delivery dates
    - Changes to orders (more, or less, items now required)
    - Involvement of departments or staff members not previously required by the project
    - Additional communications, or presentations, to the customer base for information and/or reassurance

- o Change reporting frequency
- o Introduce a new meetings schedule
- What processes or standards are needed for each option:
  - Bespoke development work
  - Design from scratch
  - Contracted out
  - Use company staff
  - Modify current product
  - Hire in contract staff
  - Modify a bought-in product
  - Buy a ready-made solution
- Who is going to take the actions:
  - Explicitly state any changes to the organisational structure
- When are the actions to be implemented:
  - If steps cannot be taken immediately, explain why this is not possible, eg, lead times for ordering supplies
- Advantages and disadvantages:
  - For each option, the key advantages and disadvantages should be listed

Keep the complexity of the Exception Report relevant to the complexity of the issue. If the issue is straightforward, but it is being escalated to the Project Board because it will take the budget for the stage out of tolerance, keep the Exception Report simple. If the issue is very complex, with multiple knock-on effects, then the information set out above should be included.

In proposing options, you must give consideration to the environment in which you are working. In other words, think about the way in which the project is being approached, the priorities of the Senior User and others on the Project Board. What are the key priorities – keeping within budget, delivering on time, attaining all the quality criteria for the products? To get the required authorisation from the Project Board, it is necessary to:

- Deal with the issue
- Provide options that are palatable to the Project Board

One of the options that must always be considered is to do nothing. Having investigated the amount of time, money and other resources required to fix the problem, it might be possible to recommend acceptance of the situation and no further action.

Request for Exception Plan

PRINCE2 states that the Exception Report must be sent to each member of the Project Board. They might not necessarily meet to select a preferred action, there may just be communication between the members to confirm that an Exception Plan is required for one of the options.

Once an Exception Plan has been created and authorised, the actions within it will be carried out in the same way as 'taking corrective action', ie, a new Work Package will be undertaken to fix the issue.

Premature closure

If the issue has a significant effect on the Business Case for the project, the Project Board may feel they have no other option than to recommend premature closure. Even if this was the most obvious or the only solution to the issue, you do not have the authority to authorise premature closure, this must come from the Project Board.

Premature closure will follow the steps outlined in the process 'Closing a project', although some steps may have to be modified as the project did not complete. For example, at the point of premature closure not all products will have been created. However, there may be some items that can be accepted by the customer, and these may also require operations and maintenance handover. The development of the Follow-On Actions Report may take significantly longer than for a standard project closure, as everything still left to do and the estimates and plans associated with the work should not be wasted but should be incorporated in this document for future use.

The Lessons Learned Report is an important document for examining why the project has been prematurely closed. Could the issue that led to the premature closure have been identified during start-up or initiation? Should the probability and consequences of the issue have been identified, and therefore actions planned which would have tackled the issue?

Reporting on issues

In reporting to the Project Board (Highlight Reports), it is important to keep them up to date on the status of issues.

At the end of each stage, a summary of all issues received during the stage and what has happened to them is included in the End Stage Report.

As part of the End Stage Assessment, the Project Board will check to see that issues have been raised for any products not delivered during the stage, and that there is a statement of the action to be taken.

After examining the issue and gathering data, the Stage Plan should be reviewed by finalising the options on how the issue should be handled. This review should cover not just the effects of the issue in terms of time but also on the budget and other resources that have been allocated to the stage. If there is a Change Budget for this project, then the cost of each option for dealing with the issue should be reviewed against this, to see if the funds are available and what percentage of the overall project budget the issue will require.

Another key consideration is identifying, for each option, whether or not the cost and time involved will take the stage outside of tolerance. An assessment of how much tolerance has already been used during the stage should be carried out.

Early identification and reporting of problems, together with potential solutions, indicates to the Project Board that you are in control of your project.

REQUIRED RESOURCES

Appropriate action	Required resource	Comments
Capturing Project Issues	**Who?** • Project manager • Project support • Configuration Librarian **What?** • Project Issue • Issue Log • Filing structure	Even misunderstandings and questions should be logged, then answered, and then closed. This will provide a trace for future questions and audit.
Examining Project Issues	**Who?** • Project manager • Team managers • Project Board • Specialist teams **What?** • Issue Log • Project Issue • Stage Plan • Team plans • Product Descriptions • Information from teams • Planning tools	Ensure that you involve the appropriate people when examining Project Issues. Not only will you save time, but there might be impacts on other products or projects that need identifying. This process should be done as quickly as possible, so gaining the help of others is important.
Reviewing stage status	**Who?** • Project manager **What?** • Stage Plan • Team plans • Checkpoint Reports • Issue Log • Risk Log	You should carry out this process on a regular basis – not just when a Project Issue is raised. There will always be times when a fresh perspective is needed. Use all the information you have available to you and step back to view the entire stage. This will help you to identify potential problems, and also where things are working well.

Continued overleaf

REQUIRED RESOURCES

Appropriate action	Required resource	Comments
Taking corrective action	**Who?** • Project manager • Teams • Project support **What?** • Issue Log • Stage Plan • Work Package	When planning additional work, or changes to current work, you should involve the teams who are working on that piece of work so that a full assessment of achievement to date can be established and used as a form of baseline for future work planned. This will help not to waste what has been done to date, and also help prevent the problems from re-occurring.
Escalating Project Issues	**Who?** • Project manager • Project Board **What?** • Issue Log • Analysis information • Exception Report	Speed is the key when escalating issues. The vehicle for escalating a Project Issue is the Exception Report. When planning the controls during Initiation, you should think carefully about the format of the Exception Report. Verbal or email Exception Reporting will often be more appropriate when impacts are great. You will already have the data from the process 'Examining Project Issues', and therefore can summarise this quickly to the Project Board. Likewise, the Project Board needs to give a speedy response as the project manager is technically not authorised to continue when in exception.
Reporting issues	**Who?** • Project manager • Team manager **What?** • Issue Log • Highlight Report • End Stage Report • Exception Report	Keep a close eye on the Issue Log as open Project Issues may change in status. It is all too easy to lose sight of issues that you feel have already been dealt with, but that have not been closed. Teams from suppliers might already be reporting on issues directly to the Project Board (via the Senior Supplier)

Chapter 11

Towards the End of a Stage

OVERVIEW

The End of a Stage is a vital point as it is an opportunity to submit all the work to date to the Project Board for their approval and gain further authorisation and commitment to work that is about to be undertaken. It is an important step in moving the project forward. In particular, the End Stage Report will encourage the Project Board (Senior User) in effect to 'sign off' the products that have been created.

APPROPRIATE ACTIONS

This chapter covers a number of activities that must be undertaken so that the end of the stage is used as effectively as possible; in particular:

- End Stage reporting
- Noting lessons learned
- Presenting progress to senior management

End Stage reporting

At the end of each management stage, an End Stage Report must be written which explains how the stage was completed. Information can be used from the:

- Current Stage Plan
- Issue Log, Highlight & Checkpoint Reports

- Next Stage Plan
- Project Plan
- Business Case
- Risk Log

The report must be kept as simple as possible. The first section will report on the stage that is completing. The Project Board will have been aware, if not involved with the events of the stage; so don't bother trying to paint a pretty picture. Be blunt and factual. Use a bullet point structure; it will help stop you waffling, and will be easier to read for the Project Board. Summarise situations that occurred and give either the result of events or their current status. Avoid giving just half of a story. The section should include performance on:

- Organisation
- Products
- Time
- Cost

All the above should be measured against the approved plan so that the Project Board has objective information on how the stage was carried out. You should report on the major events within the stage, including the reasons for any actions taken that were in addition to the approved plan.

You will have created the next Stage Plan as part of the current stage, and you therefore need to show what impact that plan has on the Project Plan, Business Case and Risk Log. You should summarise these impacts in a simple table, which indicates the baseline, present, and differences.

The End Stage Report should be circulated to the Project Board members with the next Stage Plan. You should circulate these documents in advance of the End Stage Assessment (ESA) where they will be discussed. This will give everybody concerned enough time to digest the information and request modifications where necessary.

One way to consider presenting the End Stage Report and the next-Stage Plan is to create a 'Stage Initiation Document' (SID). The SID is not a PRINCE2 product, but provides a way of keeping all the information for the current situation and future in one place. The SID is structured as a 'mini PID' – and there is one for each stage.

Contents might include:

- End Stage Report
  - Achievements to date
  - Project Plan review
  - Business Case review
  - Risk review
- Next Stage Plan
  - Incorporating Stage Quality Plan
- Stage organisation structure
- Summary of controls for stage

The main benefit of this approach is that a SID provides one reference document for the current situation/next Stage Plan, effectively providing a baseline to act as a marker, which clearly indicates value and achievement to date.

Noting lessons learned

As part of a structured approach to your project, it's a good idea to capture any useful lessons that become apparent as the project progresses. This will provide you with a store of data on which to reflect at the end of the project. It will also help to identify any trends or themes (good or bad) running through the project, and enable you to take action on them and stop them becoming issues.

Make sure that the document is easy to update – you will be learning lessons during the busiest time of the project, so you do not have time to create fancy documents. Identify an easy way to keep notes as you go forward. For example, always keep a notepad in your drawer for recording items as they arise, or use a couple of back pages in your project note-book, so that the log is always with you. Another idea is to keep a simple word processing document always open on your PC, so when ideas come to you, you can just click across to the document and type them in.

As there is no immediate benefit to recording this information, it all too easily falls to the bottom of the 'to do' list. So get in the habit of scheduling five minutes each day to jot down any thoughts.

To get the most from this process, you have to make a conscious effort to do a quick 'post mortem' of how things are going. For example:

- After you have given a presentation, or attended a project presentation from one of your team members, ask the following questions:
  - Was everything communicated that was on the agenda?
    - If something was missed out, what were the reasons – run out of time, audience wanted to spend time on other items, either already on the agenda or by introducing new items?
  - Was there any part of the presentation to which the audience was unreceptive?
    - What were the reasons for this?
- When you finish chairing a project meeting, ask the following questions:
  - Was the meeting structured?
  - Was everything on the agenda covered?
  - Were there a lot of new items that were not included in the agenda?
  - Did everyone have a chance to contribute?
  - For those that did not contribute, what were the reasons for this?
- When you are reviewing stage status, ask yourself:
  - What are the reasons for any items behind schedule?
  - Is there a pattern to late-running activities? For example, does the same team carry them all out, or do they all require the involvement of the same staff members or suppliers?

- When meeting with the Senior User, users or other stakeholders in the project, ask these questions:
  - Does the audience feel fully involved in the project?
  - Are they committed to its success?
  - Are they receiving sufficient and timely information about the project?
  - Are they receiving enough information about the project?

In addition, any problems or issues that project team members draw to your attention should be reviewed for any potential lessons learned and noted, if appropriate. Remember: keep it non-personal.

Keep it non-judgemental. Describe the problem that occurred, the situation that led to it and recommendations for preventing the problem in the future.

Presenting progress to senior management

Highlight Reports give the Project Board a regular stream of progress information. However, at the end of any stage of work it is important to meet the Project Board to review with you at first hand how things have gone, to reflect on the products created so far and discuss the implications of committing resources to the next stage. This meeting is known as an End Stage Assessment.

These meetings are vital to the life of the project, as any failure to answer questions raised by the Project Board could at best lead cause a delay while information is provided, or, at worst, lead to premature closure of the project.

The key objective of your preparation for the meeting must be to identify potential areas of interest/questions from the Project Board, and make sure you present them with all the relevant information before or during the End Stage Assessment. Do not be caught out by any failure in your preparation. Take this meeting seriously and prepare for it. This applies even if the stage has gone perfectly to plan and expenditure is exactly on budget – the Project Board will still have questions.

While it is usually the project manager who undertakes the preparation for the meeting, it is the Executive who chairs it. This puts the project manager in a difficult position, because the project manager has to gain the Executive's support for the agenda and ensure that it is closely followed.

There are three key areas to address when presenting progress:

- Preparation in advance of the End Stage Assessment
- Behaviour and actions during the End Stage Assessment
- Follow-up from the End Stage Assessment

Preparation in advance of the End Stage Assessment

The overall purpose of the meeting is to ensure the customer is happy with the products produced so far and get agreement to the next stage of the project. To ensure that you achieve this:

- Create an agenda that can be reviewed and agreed with the Executive
- Send out information in advance of the meeting
- This will give members of the Project Board an opportunity to review the agenda and read the End Stage Report. Hopefully, they will also review the next Stage Plan, so it might be worth highlighting any areas of work that require staff and resources from departments under the responsibility of the Senior User or Senior Supplier
- Identify the meeting attendees
- Just like for any party, people hate to be left off the guest list.

Typically, people only remember 20% of what they hear, 30% of what they read and about 50% of what they hear and read.

The presentation can be based on the contents of the End Stage Report. Therefore, the structure will include milestone reporting. Create a high-level Gantt chart that shows only the milestones, their planned and actual delivery dates. Provide a line of commentary to explain any early or late deliveries.

Statistics and graphical representation of data are useful and easier to understand. The key advantage of using graphs is that they can convey considerable information in a small space.

Information should include:

- financial reporting
- key items from the Risk Log
- all high-impact/high-probability risks
- all risks relevant to the next stage
- significant risks that are no longer a risk
  - Explain what changes in the situation have led to them no longer being a risk
- quality statistics
  - Be prepared to explain any products that have gone through more than a couple of quality checks
- investment appraisal
  - one-page investment appraisal from the Business Case
    - Highlight figures that have changed since the last End Stage Assessment
      - Give explanations
      - Do not say anything that you cannot support with evidence. After all, whatever your opinion, it was formed from sources of information, so make sure they are to hand.

The progress part of the presentation should be structured so that it leads onto the presentation of what is to be achieved in the next stage. So, in planning the contents, think about the key issues for the stage ahead and work backwards.

That is not to say that the progress aspect is less important, but the Project Board have been receiving regular progress reports and this is their first opportunity to review the next Stage Plan and work through the implications of committing further resources to the project.

For each End Stage Assessment, the resources being committed can come from a wide variety of areas, so sometimes they may be under the control of the Senior User or the Senior Supplier. Also, if significant resources are coming from a particular department it might be a good idea to have a line manager invited to be on hand to answer any questions regarding staff involvement.

Behaviour and actions during the End Stage Assessment

You should consider trying to set the meeting environment prior to the End Stage Assessment and should remember to always:

- act managerially
- present the information
- be truthful
- be proud of your successes

Your attitude can set the tone at the meeting. Acting positively will help to ease the senior manager's mood. Information should be presented in a clear and logical way, so you should prepare carefully for the meeting. Also, be truthful – the meeting is intended to ensure that everybody is aware, and fully understands the current situation.

Be honest about difficulties ahead. This will encourage the Project Board to become involved and give assistance when you walk them through the complexities of the next stage.

When presenting technical information don't forget that you may need to translate it into non-technical language that everyone can understand. The Senior Supplier may be able to assist during this part of the presentation. Alternatively, have any relevant members of the project team available at the meeting to take part in the presentation or simply to answer questions at the end.

You will capture the interest of the Senior User if you report on the products created in the stage by user priority rather than in the sequence in which they were created. Start with the highest priority; this has the advantage of not only making your presentation relevant to the Senior User, but gives an impression of focus on the product delivery, rather than the more standard 'on schedule, on budget' approach.

Answer the questions but:

- Do not give excuses
- Do not be evasive
  - If you have not got the information, agree to follow up later (and set a date for a further meeting) but remember that you want to prevent the issue becoming a sticking point that holds up agreement in the meeting.

Follow-up from the End Stage Assessment

Take five minutes to review the meeting. Ask such questions as:

- What were the key areas of concern from individual members of the Project Board?

- Was the length of the meeting appropriate for all the areas to be covered?

- Were topics covered that would have been handled offline better with an individual Project Board member (perhaps in advance of the meeting next time)?

- Were topics covered that would have been better addressed by a written report, or graphical representation (perhaps in the information pack sent out before the meeting)?

- Were there any questions that you or your team felt unable to answer, or answered badly? What information should you have brought with you to overcome this?

Senior managers do not enjoy having their time wasted, so don't forget to review the administration of the event and identify any improvements. For example, such simple things as:

- Was everyone clear on the time and location of the meeting, or did some people have to be chased to attend?
- Was the meeting room suitable?

REQUIRED RESOURCES

Appropriate action	Required resource	Comments
End Stage Report	**Who?** • Project manager • Project Assurance • Project Support **What?** • Stage Plan • Issue Log • Quality Log • Highlight Reports • Next Stage Plan • Project Plan • Business Case • Risk Log	When pulling together the End Stage Report you might find it useful for project support to assemble the various pieces of information into a more readable format for the Project Board. Project Assurance should at least receive a copy of the ESR in order to confirm its accuracy.
Noting lessons learned	**Who?** • Project manager **What?** • Daily Log • Project Issues	If you do not keep a Lessons Learned Log, then at least keep an area in the Daily Log that can be reviewed and summarised easily at Stage End.
Presenting progress to senior management	**Who?** • Project manager • Project Board **What?** • End Stage Report • Next Stage Plan • Agenda • Presentation	It is a good idea to involve the Senior User when preparing for the End Stage Assessment. This might help you to predict any problem areas that might arise from the customer/user side at the meeting.

Part 4

Closing a project

Chapter 12

Delivering final products

OVERVIEW

On completing a project there are two elements of acceptance — customer and maintenance. The customer will need to sign off the project outcome against the Acceptance Criteria established during start-up, and there will need to be a controlled handover and acceptance by the operational units with agreement that the product(s) can be maintained in operational life.

APPROPRIATE ACTIONS
Arranging operations handover

An integral part of successfully closing the project is the acceptance of the products by those responsible for their ongoing maintenance or support. Also, it is important to tell any areas of the business affected by changes created by the project when the products will go live. For example, these areas of business might include audit departments, quality departments, finance, etc.

These tasks must be completed before the project closes, because it is at that point that the project management team is likely to disband and the significant product knowledge that has been developed will be lost.

It might be worth ensuring that tasks related to handover are included in the Project Plan and resources assigned to them. This will help to determine at the outset that what is to be undertaken within the project life cycle and so ensure that future issues are dealt with by operations.

Steps to achieving effective handover:

- Identify all areas other than direct users involved in product adoption
- Meet with the support areas
- Plan information sessions and training sessions
- Develop training materials
- Carry out training
- Provide products in appropriate form
- Ensure that members of the project team are available for follow-up

Identify all areas other than direct users involved in product adoption

Obvious places to look for this information include those departments that support the users currently. Look for interdependencies between these departments so that any supporting information that needs forwarding is indeed done so.

Meet with the support areas

Arrange meetings with the support areas and identify their information and training needs.

Plan information sessions and training sessions

Create a plan for the training required. This plan will be a product that is accepted as part of the final deliverable. Input will be required from the area accepting the end product with regard to dates, availability etc.

Ongoing training requirements may need to be delivered by members of the project team. Look for future mandates or future business from this.

Develop training materials

Develop training materials, and any help guides or user guides. These products should have been identified during Project Planning so hopefully do not come as any surprise.

Carry out training

Carry out training specifically for the team to whom the products will be handed over. They will have different training requirements to the actual users, so this additional training is likely to be required. For example, for software and systems, this team will need to understand how to maintain and fix the products, rather than use them on a daily basis. Alternatively, if these activities have been planned far enough in advance, members of the relevant department can be seconded to the project, so that they can pick up on the job information about the products.

Provide products in appropriate form

- Hand over copies of the configuration management records with the products, so there is a complete history to each of the products.
- Provide copies of the Follow On Actions Report if it contains follow-up directly related to any of the products. For example, if the report documents known errors or omissions and the steps required to resolve them, then it should be passed on.
- Make sure all related documentation, user guides, operating instructions, etc, are handed over with the products.
- As the people receiving the products from the project will not have your knowledge of how and why they were created and how each product relates to others, it's a good idea to provide some of this information. Bear in mind that for any questions that this team cannot answer in the future, they will naturally look to the former project manager for answers.
- Clearly show dependencies and interfaces between products. Create a chart that highlights these things and take the time to walk it through with the team that the products are handed over to.

Ensure that members of the project team are available for follow-up

Ensure that members of the project team are available for follow-up and to assist with the transition of the products into operational use. It is important to schedule this activity to ensure that the project team members are still available before disbanding the project team.

Gaining customer acceptance

Gaining customer acceptance is obviously an important step to successfully completing your project. Continuous assessment of customer satisfaction will make final acceptance that much easier.

Within PRINCE2 you have a number of quality criteria and sign-offs:

- Project Brief
  - Acceptance Criteria
  - Customer's quality expectations
    - Signed off during authorising initiation
- Project Initiation Document
  - Acceptance Criteria
  - Quality Plan
  - High-level Product Descriptions (with quality criteria)
    - Signed off when PID is approved after initiation
- Stage Plans
  - Product Descriptions (with quality criteria)
  - Quality Plan
  - Quality review information
  - Identified reviewers
    - Signed off at End Stage Assessment
- End Stage Report
  - Confirmation that all products from stage were reviewed & signed off
    - Signed off at End Stage Assessment (by Senior User)
- Work Packages
  - Product Descriptions (with quality criteria)
  - Quality checking method to be used
  - Quality checking arrangements
    - Signed off by project manager when Work Package is returned

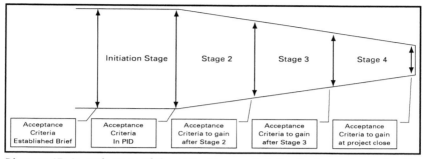

Diagram 17: As each stage of the project is accepted, the final acceptance should naturally become less daunting

- Product Descriptions
  - Quality criteria
  - Format
  - Quality method (checking)
  - Quality skills required
    - Signed off by reviewers/quality review chair

As you can see from the extensive list above, acceptance throughout your project is happening all the time. By tracking this acceptance, you can make final customer acceptance more straightforward.

Diagram 17 demonstrates progressive customer acceptance. As you can see, at the start of the project, you should agree acceptance criteria with the customer. This will be documented initially in the Project Brief, and then taken forward to the PID. The ideal way to establish acceptance criteria is to get the customer to state what it will take for them to accept the final outcome. This way there can be no misunderstanding!

As each product is assessed against the agreed quality criteria at quality review, it is returned to the configuration library where its status is changed to 'approved'. This means that the product cannot change without going through change control (and through the Project Board).

At the end of the stage, all products are signed off by the Project

Board, and in particular by the Senior User. It is at this point that you should discuss the acceptance criteria with the Senior User to determine what has been achieved to date against the criteria. This can then be tracked and updated at the end of each stage. Continually assessing customer satisfaction, maintaining buy-in and goodwill will make ultimate acceptance easier.

Not only does this theory assist you with ensuring that you are on the right track, but it also keeps the customer involved at all times. The theory is good and it does work in practice.

REQUIRED RESOURCES

Appropriate action	Required resource	Comments
Arranging operations handover	**Who?** • Project manager • Operations • Senior User **What?** • PID • Product Descriptions • Configuration management system	Historical information for each of the products will be in the configuration management records that should be handed across as part of operations handover. There should also be a discussion/transfer of the risks that the project identified. Although these risks may not have occurred during the project life, some might still be a threat in operational life.
Gaining customer acceptance	**Who?** • Project manager • Senior User • Customer • Programme management **What?** • PID • Customer quality expectations • Acceptance Criteria • Quality Log	Keeping the customer informed at all times will make final acceptance easier, as will continually assessing the acceptance criteria that you are striving to meet. We have seen customer satisfaction levels higher for projects not delivering on time or to budget but that had kept the customer informed and involved throughout the project. We have also seen the reverse, where the project delivered on time and to budget, but had low customer satisfaction through non-involvement of the customer.

Chapter 13

Closing down

OVERVIEW

Towards the end of a project, you should start evaluating the project by creating an End Project Report and a Lessons Learned Report. These two reports will indicate how the project was managed and summarise the techniques and skills used. From this information, processes and methods can evolve to improve the management of future projects.

A controlled closure is essential to enable the project to close and the teams to move on. All outstanding issues should be dealt with and a post-project review should be planned to examine whether the benefits were, indeed, achieved.

APPROPRIATE ACTIONS
End Project Report

You will need the following information to complete the End Project Report:

- Baseline PID
- Lessons Learned Report
- Quality and Issue Logs

You will also need updated information on:
- Project Plan
- Business Case
- Risk Log

The End Project Report is created to report on the project to establish how well it performed against the Project Plan in initiation. You should record how the PRINCE2 Processes were performed, and whether the objectives of the project have been met. Think about how the level of the PRINCE2 Processes were tailored and scaled to meet the needs of the project.

You will be describing the changes that took place, how those changes were handled and why the decisions were taken. The impacts of such changes should be described. This information can be gathered largely from the Stage Plans and End Stage Reports.

Your original costs and timescales will need to be drawn from the baseline Business Case (held in the PID) and you should report on how those items have changed over the project life. You should outline the benefits that have been achieved to date, and the expected benefits to be gained from operational life.

Documenting lessons learned

According to PRINCE2, the purpose of the Lessons Learned Report is to pass on any lessons that can be usefully applied to other projects. The aim is that the information is used by part of the organisation (perhaps Quality Assurance or the Project Support Office) to refine, change and improve the standards related to project management.

The source for this report will be the Lessons Learned Log. This is likely to contain information in note form, almost a shorthand version of events from the perspective of the project manager. To create the report, a number of steps have to be undertaken:

- Organise the notes into categories
- Review the situations from all perspectives
- Insert background information
- Suggest future actions to be taken

Organise the notes into categories

To provide structure to the report, divide the lessons into areas of the project management affected. For example:

- Organisation structure
  - Any roles that it would have been useful to have
  - Any skills requirements needed for specific roles
- Planning
  - By comparing actual events with their planned duration and budget, are there any useful metrics that can be applied to future estimating?
- User involvement
  - Any areas where this was particularly helpful
  - Try and give examples of the benefits of user involvement. For example, good ideas put forward by users or errors that they spotted.
- Tools and techniques used
  - Provide an assessment of any tools and techniques used and how they could be better employed next time. For example, arrange for training of project staff on planning or document management software.
- Analysis of Project Issues
  - Identify any main causes of issues or any trends.
- Communication
  - Examples of good communication, where the message was well received or the accuracy of the information was particularly strong.
  - Examples of confused communication.
- Decision making
- Review process
  - Was it timely?
  - Did it lead to any delays?

Review the situations from all perspectives

Review the situations noted from a wider perspective than just the project manager. For example, try and get the 'corporate' view of any issues, as well as the views of any team members.

Insert background information

The key issue in documenting lessons learned is recognising that information previously only relevant to the project team and those directly affected by the project is now going to become available to a wider audience. Therefore, it is important to review your notes, and insert background information where applicable.

Suggest future actions to be taken

In order to ensure that problems don't arise in the future, it's a good idea to suggest ideas for how they can be overcome. Even if the company does not adopt these suggestions, it will get the ball rolling and keep the focus on improving things rather than apportioning blame.

Finishing off

To finish off a project, and finally close it down, you must identify all the things that need to be followed up. Even at the end of a successfully completed project, there may be things left undone, either because they have not been finished during the life of the project or because they are related to how the products are used in a live environment.

It is the project manager's responsibility to ensure that these ideas are documented and passed to those who have the authority and responsibility to take action. In this way they will not be lost and if appropriate they can be picked up for development by subsequent projects. Follow On Actions Recommendations are created. There are two key sources of information for identifying these follow on actions:

- *Issues Log*
  - Document all issues that remain open, or any issues that were held

as pending during the life of the project
- *Risk Log*
  - Document all risks that were identified in relation to the operational use of the products

In addition, there are a number of housekeeping tasks that should be carried out in readiness for the final closure of the project:

- *Close down cost centres associated with project*
  In large organisations, you may be allocated a cost centre number that you must quote on all payments. This enables the finance department to track where money is being spent in the company. Once the project reaches closure, and as soon as there is no longer any need for the cost centre, officially close it down and terminate your authority to sign for payments. This will minimise the risk of any false claims being processed once the project has closed.
- *Establish a release and re-assignment plan for all team members*
  For temporary staff, complete all final timesheets and arrange for payment of all final invoices.
- *Prepare appraisal forms on the performance of team members*
  If required, prepare appraisal forms on the performance of team members and send them to their line managers and/or human resources or personnel departments.
- *Arrange to archive all the project files*
  It probably is not a good idea to archive every single document that was ever written in connection with the project. PRINCE2 suggests that items of little future value should be 'weeded out', by a group consisting of the project manager, Project Assurance and Project Support. As a guideline, the future uses of the documentation will be:
  - Auditors, auditing the project's actions and performance
  - Project Support Office
  - Future project managers (for planning models, estimates etc)
  - Those carrying out the Post-Project Review.

It is also worth noting that both hard copies and soft copies of documents, presentations, designs and other information will need to be archived.

To provide a full audit trail of discussions you will want to include emails, so it might be worth printing out all the relevant correspondence from each email account, and filing it according to the item to which it relates. This may be especially important in those organisations that have a policy of disposing of all email correspondence once an email account has been closed down.

- *Create notification of dates for final reports and communications*
  Towards the end of a project, motivation levels of those involved can lessen; therefore, if there are any final reports, presentations or communications for which participation or sign-off is required, notify people of the dates when their involvement will be required. This can also be a useful opportunity to thank them for their involvement.

- *Notify relevant parties of the creation of new assets*
  Use the configuration management record to inform any relevant departments of new 'assets' that the company now has – for example someone in the company might be responsible for logging and tranching all software or equipment that the company owns.

Post-Project Review Plan

Following successful completion of the project, an assessment may be carried out to identify if all the benefits previously identified as reasons for undertaking the project have actually been achieved. (See Diagram 18.)

Typically this assessment is called a Post-Project Review or sometimes a Post-Implementation Review as it is carried out months after the project has been completed. There is no guarantee that the original project staff will be involved. Therefore it is a good idea the project manager puts together a suggested plan for how the review might be carried out, using all of his or her project knowledge. There may be information that was gathered during project creation or quality reviews

Process, general	Were standard templates used?
	Were all templates of value in this project?
	Which tools or techniques were not used?
	Were there organizational obstacles that made it difficult or impossible to use any part of the process?
Stage-specific	Was the Justification Stage completed successfully?
	Was the Planning Stage completed successfully?
	Was the Activation Stage completed successfully?
	Was the Control Stage completed successfully?
	Was the Evaluation Stage completed successfully?
Control-specific	Were communications adequate in all activities?
	Was risk controlled adequately?
	Was an adequate contingency plan created?
	Did the project meet all original scheduled milestones/deadlines?
	Was project status reported according to plan?
	Were all issues resolved in a timely manner?
	Did the change-control procedure work adequately?
	Did the project receive all the necessary approvals to proceed in a timely fashion?
	Was the project staffed appropriately?
	Was quality of the product or services adequate?

Diagram 18: Things to consider when assessing the project

that should be included in the review, which someone unconnected with the project would not know. This is only a suggested plan; it is certainly an area that should be discussed with the Project Board before undertaking, as a review is not always required.

In order to plan the review, the Business Case should be checked for:

- all benefits associated with the project
- whether the benefits are written in measurable terms (it isn't really possible to measure the success of something that provides 'better productivity,' as better can mean many different things. You need to know exactly what improvements were expected, for example, increase in productivity from 100 items an hour to 150 items an hour).
- whether measurements of the situation were taken before the project was delivered, so there is something to compare against. If information does not exist on the 'before' situation, then it is going to be extremely difficult to prove that any benefit has been achieved. This should have been identified when the Business Case was authorised as part of the Project Initiation Document, but it often gets forgotten. If you find that data does not exist, you could arrange for measurements of the situation to be taken now, ie, just before the products go live or very close to when they started being used – at best this will give you something to compare against.
- indicators of how the benefit should be measured after the project has been completed.

The Post-Project Review Plan does not need to be a schedule of activities, instead it can set out:

- the structure of what is to be reviewed
- key questions to be asked, design of how the results are to presented
- identification of who is to receive the results

The first step is to take the benefits listed in the Business Case as your starting point. Secondly, give consideration to how benefits can be measured from all angles so that as much positive data can be gathered as possible. For example, if a benefit of your project was that staff costs would fall, as fewer staff would be required to operate the new product, ensure that measures are taken relating to:

- number of staff
- costs of staff at each level of seniority
- overtime as well as salary costs

Structure of what is to be reviewed:

- Which areas of the business are to be reviewed? The obvious answer is the department into which the product was implemented. However, in order to ensure the review is comprehensive you may include departments upstream and downstream from the directly affected department.
- Who is best placed to carry out the review
  - External resources, eg, a consultancy
  - Former project resources
  - Staff from affected department
  - Staff with checking skills, eg, audit, compliance, quality assurance

Key questions to be asked:

- How well has the product achieved its benefits? You could consider grading the answer to this question – high/medium/low, As expected/less than expected/more than expected or use the traffic-light approach Red (bad)/Amber (under achieved/small differences)/Green (better or as expected).

- Trend analysis. For each benefit measured, can it be seen that there is a trend of improvement and, if so, when is this likely to peak?
- How do the users feel about the product? Consider holding feedback sessions (possibly without senior management so that true feelings can be expressed) or conducting surveys – perhaps at fixed points during the first year of implementation to provide trend analysis.
- Does the product meet quality expectations? This is always an interesting question to answer, as the user community will often identify requirements that the product does not meet, or features it does not have, once it is in use. To ensure the post-project review does not get weighed down by the creation of these wish lists (which can form the basis of a further project), the plan must make it clear that the product is being judged against the stated quality expectations.

Obviously the complexity of any post-project review, and therefore Post-Project Review Plan, will depend upon the number of benefits to be assessed, and how difficult it is to measure them. Scale the information in this section so that it is applicable to your project quality expectations that were authorised in the PID. It is important to guard against the project being evaluated against anything other than documented expectations, as this will always lead to a negative outcome. This is particularly important if the quality expectations were reduced originally when they were compared against the project budget; users can often forget that requirements were 'descoped' in order to get the project off the ground in the first place. You may evaluate:

- Is the product being supported as expected? While this question does not go directly to an evaluation of achievement of benefits, the answer can provide important data in explaining any non-achievement of benefits. If the necessary support is not available, then it is likely users will not be able to use the product to its full extent, so some value will be lost.
- Does the support staff have the materials/training to support the

product? This is an aspect of the project that should be considered when handover arrangements are created. Therefore, by including this question as part of the post-implementation review plan, it can serve as a useful reminder that arrangements for support documentation and training (if required) must be made.

- Have there been unexpected problems in the introduction of the product? Again, this is fact-finding which will put the results of the review in context. If the introduction or implementation of the product did not go according to plan it is likely that not all benefits will have been realised. Therefore, there is potential to re-schedule the review or hold it a second time at a later date to take account of delays related to teething problems.

- Has the introduction of the product caused new problems? As well as examining benefits, it is important to ensure that any new problems are identified, either as a direct result of the implementation, or as a side effect. When you are planning the review, it is a good idea to return to the Risk Log to see if any potential operational problems were identified during the project and if there were some, whether any actions to mitigate them were identified.

The review

Post-Project Reviews are not always regarded positively. It is often difficult to get excited about planning them for a variety of reasons:

- No support from both senior management and the project team to lengthen the closure process, particularly if the project was delivered late or over budget.
- No support from senior management, who only want to commit resources to a new project rather than examining the results of projects that have already completed.
- No support from the business areas affected by the project as they are so busy getting to grips with the new products that they have not got time to take part in any surveys.

- No motivation on the part of the project manager or the project team to plan something that:
  - they are unlikely to be involved in
  - may be carried out by someone who will want to plan it in their own way
  - might turn up bad news about a project which has been regarded as a success up to that point.

However, this section is written from the perspective that you are interested in ensuring that a post-project review takes place. The first step is to take the benefits listed in the Business Case as your starting point. Secondly, consider how benefits can be measured from all angles so that as much data can be gathered as possible. For example:

- If a benefit of your project was that staff costs would fall, as less staff would be required to operate the new product, ensure that measures are taken relating to:
  - number of staff
  - cost of staff at each level of seniority
  - overtime as well as salary costs

Outcome of the review

It is possible that some rework will be identified as part of a review, and that this rework will be identified as a subsequent project. Therefore, if you think this is a possibility, you can consider planning the review so that it will provide as much information as possible for the new Project Mandate.

REQUIRED RESOURCES

Appropriate action	Required resource	Comments
End Project Report	**Who?** • Project manager • Project Assurance **What?** • PID • End Stage Reports • Quality Log • Issue Log	Project Assurance can assist the project manager during the creation of the End Stage Report to: (a) ensure integrity of the contents; and (b) give feedback and information on the processes used by the entire team (including the Project Board).
Documenting lessons learned	**Who?** • Project manager • Project Assurance • Quality assurance • Teams **What?** • Lessons Learned Log • Daily Log • Project manager's diary	Consider adding a heading to the PID that details relevant Lessons Learned Reports from previous projects. This will ensure that the work carried out to document these lessons is not wasted. Where there are no relevant lessons – a disclaimer can be signed to state that this area has been considered.
Finishing off	**Who?** • Project manager • Project support • Senior User **What?** • PID • Issue Log • Quality Log	
Post-Project Review Plan	**Who?** • Project manager • Project Board Executive • Customer/users • Project support **What?** • PID • Operations information	When planning the Post-Project Review, ensure that the Executive is aware of the purpose of the meeting. The rest of the project team may not be available for the review. Nevertheless, the Executive is responsible for the benefits being achieved, and this responsibility extends to beyond the project life cycle.

And finally …

Appendix A

Key Document Maps

Business Case

Business Case
Explains the benefits of undertaking and continuing the project. Also gives financial information about the project.
Source
As a default, created at pre-project. This would normally be by way of a Feasibility Study.
Format
Document

Info from
• Feasibility Study
• Programme Plan
• Project Mandate
• Project Approach
Advice from
• Programme Management

Info from
•Programme Plan
•Project Plan
•Team Plans
•Estimating
Advice from
•Strategy Group
•Finance Group
•User Group

Info from
•Plans
•Estimating
Advice from
•Suppliers
•Teams

Business Case

Options

Benefits

Risks

Costs & Timescales

Investment Appraisal

This should be just a summary of the key risks that have been identified.
Info from
• Risk Log (Project Brief)
• Programme Risk Log
Advice from
• Programme Management
• Teams

Advice!
Although the financial information should be included within the Business Case, it is often more appropriate to keep separate for commercial reasons.

Checkpoint Report

Info from
•Previous reports
•Team Plan
•Quality Log
Advice from
•Teams
•Config Librarian

Checkpoint Report
Summary current
period of technical
Work – Work
Package report.
Frequency
As agreed with the
Project Manager
Format
Document
Email
Meeting
Verbal

Checkpoint Report

This should include
all the products that
have been completed
and summarise the
activities have been
undertaken.

Follow-ups from previous period

Work completed during period

Summarising the
quality checks that
have been completed
Info from
•Quality Log
•Product Checklist
Advice from
•Teams
•Quality Reviewers
•Project Assurance
Quality Assurance

Quality work carried out during period

Advice!
You will need to
explain the work
which will be
undertaken during the
next reporting period.
You should use the
Team Plans to
identify this work,
also the overall Stage
Plan. It is also good
practice to keep an
eye on other teams
and "Business as
usual" work to
anticipate potential
problems.

Actual/potential problems

Planned for next period

Info from
•Issue Log
•Quality Log
•Quality Review
Results
Advice from
•Senior Supplier
•Reviewers
Teams

Communication Plan

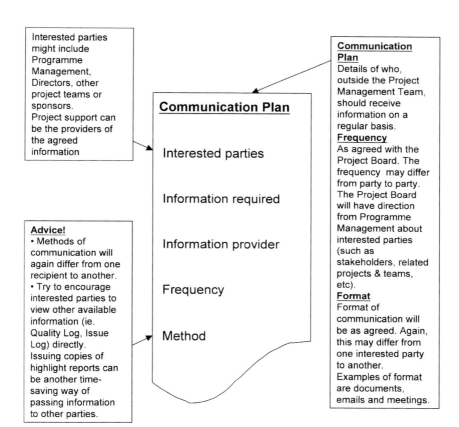

Interested parties might include Programme Management, Directors, other project teams or sponsors. Project support can be the providers of the agreed information

Communication Plan

Interested parties

Information required

Information provider

Frequency

Method

Communication Plan
Details of who, outside the Project Management Team, should receive information on a regular basis.
Frequency
As agreed with the Project Board. The frequency may differ from party to party. The Project Board will have direction from Programme Management about interested parties (such as stakeholders, related projects & teams, etc).
Format
Format of communication will be as agreed. Again, this may differ from one interested party to another. Examples of format are documents, emails and meetings.

Advice!
• Methods of communication will again differ from one recipient to another.
• Try to encourage interested parties to view other available information (ie. Quality Log, Issue Log) directly. Issuing copies of highlight reports can be another time-saving way of passing information to other parties.

Configuration Management Plan

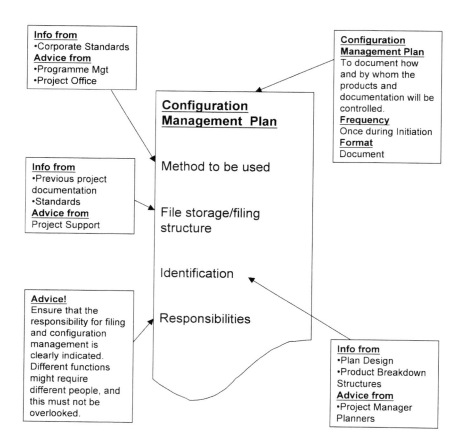

End Project Report

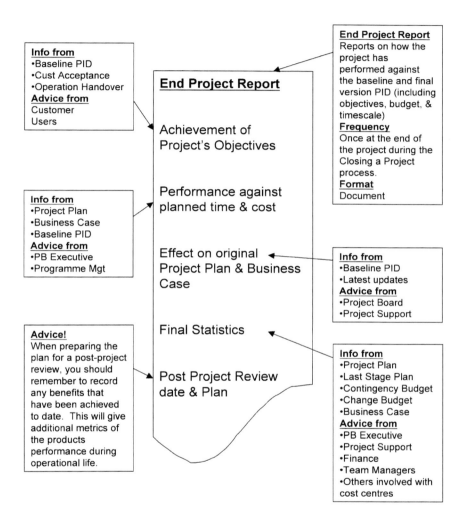

Info from
•Baseline PID
•Cust Acceptance
•Operation Handover
Advice from
Customer
Users

Info from
•Project Plan
•Business Case
•Baseline PID
Advice from
•PB Executive
•Programme Mgt

Advice!
When preparing the plan for a post-project review, you should remember to record any benefits that have been achieved to date. This will give additional metrics of the products performance during operational life.

End Project Report

Achievement of Project's Objectives

Performance against planned time & cost

Effect on original Project Plan & Business Case

Final Statistics

Post Project Review date & Plan

End Project Report
Reports on how the project has performed against the baseline and final version PID (including objectives, budget, & timescale)
Frequency
Once at the end of the project during the Closing a Project process.
Format
Document

Info from
•Baseline PID
•Latest updates
Advice from
•Project Board
•Project Support

Info from
•Project Plan
•Last Stage Plan
•Contingency Budget
•Change Budget
•Business Case
Advice from
•PB Executive
•Project Support
•Finance
•Team Managers
•Others involved with cost centres

End Stage Report

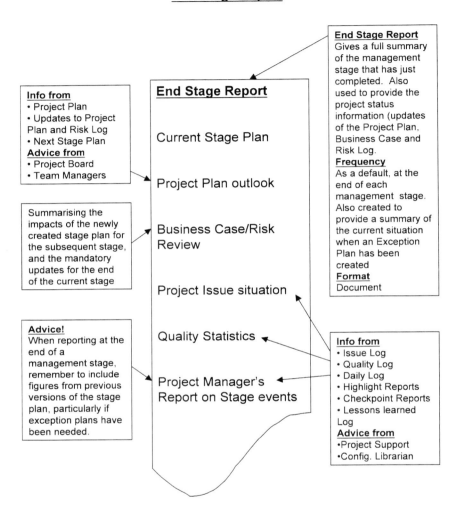

End Stage Report
Gives a full summary of the management stage that has just completed. Also used to provide the project status information (updates of the Project Plan, Business Case and Risk Log.
Frequency
As a default, at the end of each management stage. Also created to provide a summary of the current situation when an Exception Plan has been created
Format
Document

Info from
• Project Plan
• Updates to Project Plan and Risk Log
• Next Stage Plan
Advice from
• Project Board
• Team Managers

Summarising the impacts of the newly created stage plan for the subsequent stage, and the mandatory updates for the end of the current stage

Advice!
When reporting at the end of a management stage, remember to include figures from previous versions of the stage plan, particularly if exception plans have been needed.

End Stage Report

Current Stage Plan

Project Plan outlook

Business Case/Risk Review

Project Issue situation

Quality Statistics

Project Manager's Report on Stage events

Info from
• Issue Log
• Quality Log
• Daily Log
• Highlight Reports
• Checkpoint Reports
• Lessons learned Log
Advice from
•Project Support
•Config. Librarian

Exception Report

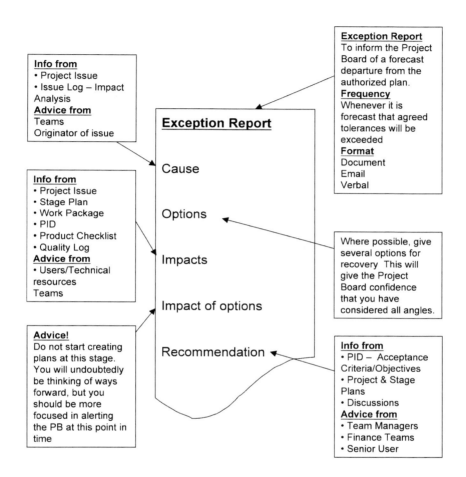

Exception Report
To inform the Project Board of a forecast departure from the authorized plan.
Frequency
Whenever it is forecast that agreed tolerances will be exceeded
Format
Document
Email
Verbal

Info from
• Project Issue
• Issue Log – Impact Analysis
Advice from
Teams
Originator of issue

Info from
• Project Issue
• Stage Plan
• Work Package
• PID
• Product Checklist
• Quality Log
Advice from
• Users/Technical resources
Teams

Advice!
Do not start creating plans at this stage. You will undoubtedly be thinking of ways forward, but you should be more focused in alerting the PB at this point in time

Exception Report

Cause

Options

Impacts

Impact of options

Recommendation

Where possible, give several options for recovery This will give the Project Board confidence that you have considered all angles.

Info from
• PID – Acceptance Criteria/Objectives
• Project & Stage Plans
• Discussions
Advice from
• Team Managers
• Finance Teams
• Senior User

Highlight Report

Highlight Report
Summary of the period of work completed since the last Highlight Report and the current status of the Management Stage.
Frequency
As agreed with the Project Board
Format
Document
Email
Meeting
Verbal

Info from
• Stage Plan
• Checkpoints
• Business Case
Advice from
Finance Teams

Highlight Report

Budget status

Info from
• Stage Plan
• Product Checklist
Advice from
• Programme (other projects)
Teams

Schedule status

Products completed

Info from
• Product Checklist
• Checkpoint Report
• Quality Log
Advice from
• Team Manager
Teams

Actual problems

Advice!
Do not include information on the whole stage. Reference points such as risks and issues rather that giving full explanation.

Period covered

Info from
• Issue Log
• Risk Log
• Daily Log
Advice from
• Senior User
Teams

Issue Log

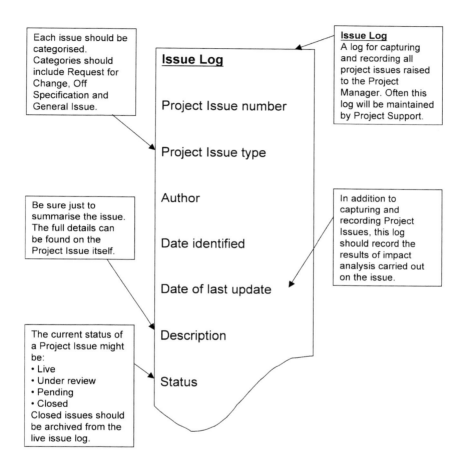

Off Specification

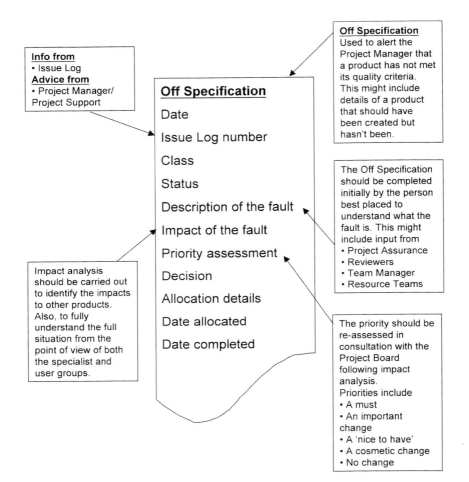

Info from
- Issue Log

Advice from
- Project Manager/
Project Support

Off Specification
Used to alert the
Project Manager that
a product has not met
its quality criteria.
This might include
details of a product
that should have
been created but
hasn't been.

Off Specification

Date

Issue Log number

Class

Status

Description of the fault

Impact of the fault

Priority assessment

Decision

Allocation details

Date allocated

Date completed

The Off Specification
should be completed
initially by the person
best placed to
understand what the
fault is. This might
include input from
- Project Assurance
- Reviewers
- Team Manager
- Resource Teams

Impact analysis
should be carried out
to identify the impacts
to other products.
Also, to fully
understand the full
situation from the
point of view of both
the specialist and
user groups.

The priority should be
re-assessed in
consultation with the
Project Board
following impact
analysis.
Priorities include
- A must
- An important
change
- A 'nice to have'
- A cosmetic change
- No change

Product Checklist

Product Checklist
Lists the products to
be developed from a
plan.
Source
Product Breakdown
Structure
Format
List

Product Checklist

Plan identification

Product names

Planned & actual dates

• Draft ready

• Quality check

• Approval

Advice!
The Product
Checklist provides
useful information to
a number of different
people in the project
management team.
It provides a list of
products with start
and end dates which
gives a simple
summary for Project
Board meetings. The
Project Manager/
Team Manager are
provided with an easy
to follow snapshot of
forecasts, and Project
Support/
Configuration
Librarian can develop
the checklist to
incorporate the status
of each product.

Product Description

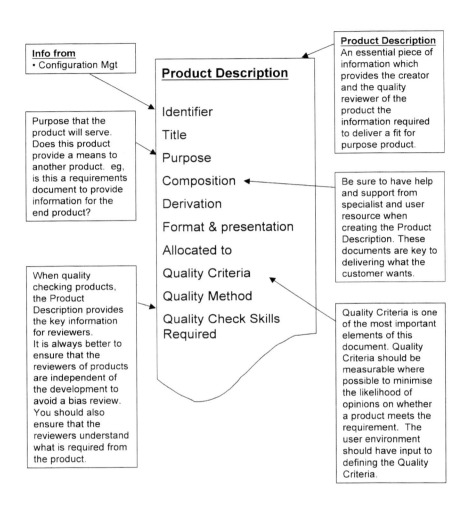

Info from
• Configuration Mgt

Product Description

Product Description
An essential piece of information which provides the creator and the quality reviewer of the product the information required to deliver a fit for purpose product.

Purpose that the product will serve. Does this product provide a means to another product. eg, is this a requirements document to provide information for the end product?

Identifier

Title

Purpose

Composition ◄

Derivation

Format & presentation

Allocated to

Quality Criteria

Quality Method

Quality Check Skills Required

Be sure to have help and support from specialist and user resource when creating the Product Description. These documents are key to delivering what the customer wants.

When quality checking products, the Product Description provides the key information for reviewers. It is always better to ensure that the reviewers of products are independent of the development to avoid a bias review. You should also ensure that the reviewers understand what is required from the product.

Quality Criteria is one of the most important elements of this document. Quality Criteria should be measurable where possible to minimise the likelihood of opinions on whether a product meets the requirement. The user environment should have input to defining the Quality Criteria.

Project Approach

Project Approach
Used to state the
approach that will be
taken to provide the
solution.
Source
Information for this
document might
come from a
feasibility study or
investigation on
examining different
options.
Format
Usually a document

Project Approach

Description of approach

Type of solution

Reasons for approach

Information on the
decision of the
approach could be
included in this
document. Topics
that should be
considered are:
• industry standards
that should be
observed for
providing a solution
• Operations/
maintenance
implications
• Training
requirements
• Interfaces with other
projects
• Technical
implications
impacting on solution

Examples are:
• Bought 'off the shelf'
• Develop 'in-house'
• Contracted out
• Partnership
• Develop existing
product
• Build from scratch

Project Brief

A brief explanation of how the project fits into the overall strategy

Defining the projects objectives. What is to be achieved? Also used to define the scope of the project to establish what is included and what is not.

At this stage the business case may just consist of outline costs and timescales for the intended project. Also, a high-level summary of expected benefits will suffice. If more information is available as a result of a feasibility study, the all the better.

Project Brief

Background

Definition

Outline Business Case

Customer's quality expectations

Acceptance criteria

Any known risks

Project Brief
Used to expand the information from the Project Mandate in order to establish essentially a 'Terms of Reference' for the project. The Project Brief will provide information to be taken into the Project Initiation Document.
Source
Project Mandate
Feasibility Report
Business/Customer
Format
Document

Your main source for establishing what the customer expects is the customer. These expectations can form part of the acceptance criteria. Again, establish what needs to be in place for the customer to ultimately accept the outcome of the project.

It is useful to use a standard risk checklist at this stage to ensure that all areas of potential risk are at least considered.

Project Initiation Document

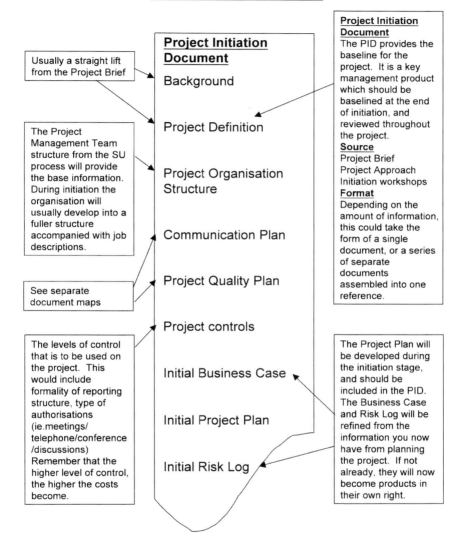

Usually a straight lift from the Project Brief

The Project Management Team structure from the SU process will provide the base information. During initiation the organisation will usually develop into a fuller structure accompanied with job descriptions.

See separate document maps

The levels of control that is to be used on the project. This would include formality of reporting structure, type of authorisations (ie.meetings/ telephone/conference /discussions) Remember that the higher level of control, the higher the costs become.

Project Initiation Document

Background

Project Definition

Project Organisation Structure

Communication Plan

Project Quality Plan

Project controls

Initial Business Case

Initial Project Plan

Initial Risk Log

Project Initiation Document
The PID provides the baseline for the project. It is a key management product which should be baselined at the end of initiation, and reviewed throughout the project.
Source
Project Brief
Project Approach
Initiation workshops
Format
Depending on the amount of information, this could take the form of a single document, or a series of separate documents assembled into one reference.

The Project Plan will be developed during the initiation stage, and should be included in the PID. The Business Case and Risk Log will be refined from the information you now have from planning the project. If not already, they will now become products in their own right.

Project Quality Plan

Info from
- Project Brief

Advice from
- Senior Supplier

Identification of the key personnel responsible for quality matters and responsibilities defined for each.

Usually derived from the quality management system requirements.

Explain how project issues will be handled. This might refer to the PRINCE2 Change Control technique, or a technique already in place within the QMS.

See separate document map.

Project Quality Plan

Customer quality expectations

Acceptance criteria

Quality responsibilities

Reference to standards

Quality control and audit process

Change management procedures

Configuration Mgt Plan

Tools to ensure quality

Project Quality Plan
To define the quality standards, processes and techniques to be used by the project in order to ensure that quality levels are achieved.
Source
Organisation standards (such as ISO or QMS/quality policy).
Format
Document

A summary of the organisation's technical/specialist standards and quality management standards which must be adhered to and reflected in the creation of the products. This will include both customer and supplier standards where appropriate. Industry standards, professional standards and ethical approaches must also be included

Details any tools that will be used to assist with filing, configuration mgt, testing, etc.

Work Package

Work Package

Identification of who is responsible for delivery of the work.

Description of what is to be achieved from the work.

A copy of each Product Description for each product to be developed. See separate document map for more details.

Type of quality checking to be used (e.g. sample test, visual inspection, etc)

In many cases, the extract of the stage plan will be the original team plan that the Team Manager would have created.

Frequency of Checkpoint Reports – see separate document map for more details.

Work Package

Team or person authorised

Work Package descr.

Product description(s)

Techniques/processes

Interfaces

Quality check method

Configuration mgt requirements

Stage Plan extract

Agreement on effort, cost, start & end dates

Sign-off requirements

Return arrangements

How completion is to be advised

Independent quality-checking arrangements

Reporting requirements

Problem handling & escalation

Work Package
Created to include all the information required to formally pass a piece of work from the Project Manager to the Team Manager in order to produce one or more products.
Once assembled, the Work Package can be authorised to the relevant Team Manager.
Format
Document

Interfaces with Project Support with regard to status of products.

All of this information should be within the Work Package, but agreed at the authorisation with the Team Manager. These headings refer to the Work Package itself. Tolerance on time and cost should also be included.

This should be derived from the Project Quality Plan.

Appendix B

PRINCE2 Process Model

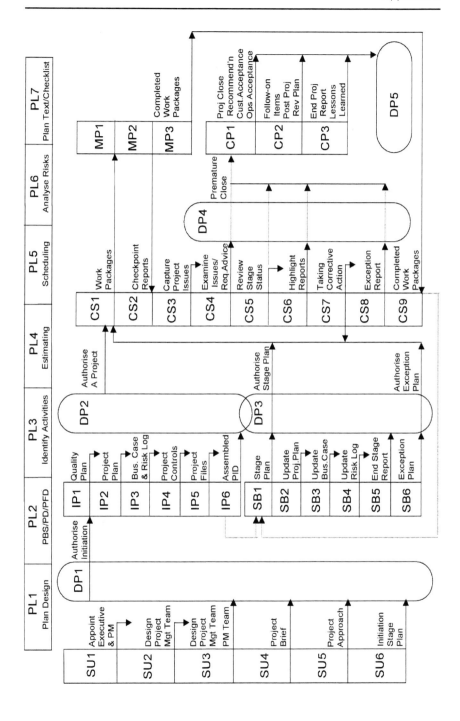

Appendix C

Suggested filing structure

Management File

This appendix gives a detailed breakdown of the PRINCE2 suggested filing structure. It is important to remember that this filing structure is recommended, and not mandatory.

Some projects, particularly smaller projects, might need just a specified directory structure stated within the project's PID. Other projects will need a more detailed breakdown of Management and Specialist product storage.

If your organisation already has filing structures in place, then there should be no reason to deviate from that standard.

Organisation File

- Organisation structure chart
- Signed job definitions for each participant
- Draft job definitions – keep each version
- CVs
- Interview notes
- Notes of discussions with:
  - Job agencies
  - Line managers
  - Human resources

If you have managerial responsibility for team members then you will need to keep the standard personnel files for all employees. However, even if staff are seconded to you, you may need to keep the following:

- Copies of exclusions to working time directive
- Holiday forms
- Sickness forms
- Appraisal forms

Plans

Each version of the Project Plan needs to be kept. Clearly divide the plan into its constituent parts as different people will want access to different parts, eg, team managers may find Product Breakdown Structures useful, but users may just want a presentation or summary version of the plan.

Different sections will include:

- Product Breakdown Structure
- Product Flow Diagrams
- Network diagrams
- Gantt charts
- Resource estimates
- Summary plans and presentation versions
  - Throughout the life of the project there will be numerous presentations of the plan for which extracts and summaries will need to be created.

Keep a note of the reasons for changes to each version. Include details such as:

- Change
- Reason for change:
  - Resource availability
  - Progress not according to plan (faster or slower than planned)
  - Change of assumptions

- Change of scope
- Result of fixing a Project Issue
- Knock-on effect of change

Project definition documentation

- Project Mandate
- Project Brief
- Project Approach
- Project Initiation Document
- Business Case initial version and all subsequent versions

Project Board communications

- Project Board approval for initiation
- Project Board approval for the project
- Record of End Stage Assessments
- Record of Mid Stage Assessments
- Project start notification
- Project end notification

Reporting

- Highlight Reports
- Lessons Learned Log
- Project closure recommendation
- Post-Implementation Review Plan
- End Project Report

Financial records

- Project budget
- Expense report

Risks

- Risk Log
- Contingency plans
- Back-out plans

Administration

For each stage of the project, create a separate file. As each stage is completed, this file can then be tied off, leaving you with only one current stage file at any one time.

Stage organisation file

- Organisation structure chart for the stage
- List of work assignments handed to each team member
- Assessment of work performance for each team member

Plans

- Stage plan
- Team plans
- Exception plans

Work to be completed in the stage

- Work Packages
- Work Package acceptances from team managers
- Any contractual documentation associated with the Work Package

Reporting

- Checkpoint Reports
- Exception Reports
- Notes from meetings and informal discussions

End Stage Assessment

- Information pack sent to each Project Board member prior to the meeting
- Presentation pack used during End Stage Assessment
- Minutes from the End Stage Assessment

Exception assessments

- For each exception assessment that is held, there should be a separate file, which includes:

- Exception Report
- Exception Plan
- Presentation pack used during the exception assessment
- Minutes from the exception assessment

Administration

Records of bookings for travel and accommodation

Specialist File

All documentation related to the creation of the deliverables from the project should be held in this file. If there are large numbers of products then consider having a separate file for each product. The file should include:

- Correspondence
  - When discussions are held between team members about the best way to do things, it is unlikely that anyone is taking notes of what was said. However, once the discussions have been concluded, try and get some record of the options that were discussed, the pros and cons of each option, and why the chosen option was the preferred way forward)
- Quotes
- Estimates
- Requests for information
- Requests for proposals
- Invitations to tender
- Draft contracts

Appendix D

Glossary

Acceptance Criteria

A prioritised list of criteria that the final product(s) must meet before the customer will accept them; a measurable definition of what must be done for the final product to be acceptable to the customer. The criteria should be defined as part of the Project Brief and agreed between customer and supplier no later than the project initiation stage. They should be documented in the Project Initiation Document.

Activity Network

A flow diagram showing the activities in a plan, and their inter-dependencies. The network shows each activity's duration; earliest start and finish times; latest start and finish times; and float. See also 'critical path'.

Ad Hoc Direction

Advice and guidance passed from the Project Board to the project manager.

Approach

See 'Project Approach'.

Assurance

See 'Project Assurance'.

Baseline

The agreed starting-point for a product (including management products). Although the position may be updated later, the baseline remains unchanged and available as a reminder of the original state and as a comparison against the current position. Products that have passed their quality checks and are approved are baselined products. Anything 'baselined' should be under version control in configuration management and 'frozen', ie, no changes to that version are allowed.

Benefits

The positive outcomes, quantified or unquantified, that a project is being undertaken to deliver, and that justify the investment.

Benefits Realisation

The practice of ensuring that the outcome of a project produces the projected benefits claimed in the Business Case.

Board

See 'Project Board'.

Breakdown Structure

See 'Product Breakdown Structure'.

Brief

See 'Project Brief'.

Business Case

Information that describes the justification for setting up and continuing a PRINCE2 project. It provides the reasons (and answers the question 'Why?') for the project. It is updated at key points throughout the project.

Change Authority

A group to which the Project Board may delegate responsibility for the consideration of requests for change. The Change Authority is given a budget and can approve changes within that budget.

Change Budget

The money allocated to the Change Authority to be spent on authorised requests for change.

Change Control

The procedure to ensure that the processing of all Project Issues is controlled, including the submission, analysis and decision making.

Change Request

See 'Request for Change'.

Checkpoint

A team-level, time-driven review of progress, usually involving a meeting.

Checkpoint Report

A progress report of the information gathered at a checkpoint meeting, which is given by a team to the project manager and provides reporting data as defined in the Work Package.

Communication Plan

Part of the Project Initiation Document describing how the project's stakeholders and interested parties will be kept informed during the project.

Concession

An Off-Specification that is accepted by the Project Board without corrective action.

Configuration Audit

A comparison of the latest version number and status of all products shown in the configuration library records against the information held by the product authors.

Configuration Management

A discipline, normally supported by software tools, that gives management precise control over its assets (for example, the products of a project), covering planning, identification, control, status accounting and verification of the products.

Configuration Status Account

A report on the status of products. The required products can be specified by an identifier or the part of the project in which they were developed.

Contingency Budget

The amount of money required to implement a contingency plan. If the Project Board approves a contingency plan, it would normally set aside a contingency budget, which would only be called upon if the contingency plan had to be implemented.

Contingency Plan

A plan that provides an outline of decisions and measures to be taken if defined circumstances, outside the control of a PRINCE2 project, should occur.

Corporate/Programme Management

The senior group involved with the overall strategic direction of an organisation (ie, board of directors, partners, strategy committee)

Critical Path

This is the line connecting the start of a planning network with the final activity in that network through those activities with the smallest float. Often this is a line through the network connecting those activities with a zero float, ie, those activities where any delay will delay the time of the entire network.

Customer

The person or group who commissioned the work and will benefit from the end results.

Customer Acceptance

Agreement by the customer that the project has met the requirements outlined in the acceptance criteria. See 'Acceptance Criteria'.

Customer Quality Expectations

A common understanding between the customer and supplier of the link between quality, time and cost – balanced with a product that is 'fit for purpose'.

Deliverable

An item that the project has to create as part of the requirements. It may be part of the final outcome or an intermediate element on which one or more subsequent deliverables are dependent. According to the type of project, another name for a deliverable is 'product'.

Direction

See 'Ad Hoc Direction'.

Earned Value Analysis

A clear measurement of the project work accomplished. The value is usually monetary but can be expressed in any appropriate unit such as staff hours, or days.

End Project Report

A report given by the project manager to the Project Board, that confirms the handover of all products and provides an updated Business Case and an assessment of how well the project has done against its Project Initiation Document.

End Stage Assessment

The review by the Project Board and project manager of the End Stage Report to decide whether to approve the next Stage Plan (unless the last stage has now been completed). According to the size and criticality of the project, the review may be formal or informal. The approval to proceed should be documented as an important management product.

End Stage Report

A report given by the project manager to the Project Board at the end of each management stage of the project. This provides information about the project performance during the stage and the project status at stage end.

Escalation

Alerting the next level of authority to potential or actual events.

Exception

The result of a deviation beyond the tolerance levels agreed between project manager and Project Board (or between Project Board and corporate or programme management, or between a team manager and the project manager).

Exception Assessment

This is a meeting of the Project Board to approve (or reject) an Exception Plan.

Exception Plan

This is a plan that often follows an Exception Report. For a Stage Plan exception, it covers the period from the present to the end of the current stage. If the exception were at a project level, the Project Plan would be replaced.

Exception Report

A report that describes an exception, provides an analysis and options for the way forward, and identifies a recommended option. The project manager gives it to the Project Board.

Executive

The chair of the Project Board, representing the customer and owner of the Business Case. The singular individual with overall responsibility for ensuring that a project or programme meets its objectives and delivers the projected benefits. This individual should ensure that the project or programme maintains its business focus, that it has clear authority and that the work, including risks, is actively managed.

Feasibility Study

A feasibility study is an early study of a problem to assess if a solution is possible. The study will normally scope the problem, identify and explore a number of solutions and make a recommendation on what action to take. Part of the work in developing options is to calculate an outline Business Case for each as one aspect of comparison.

Flow Diagram

See 'Product Flow Diagram'.

Follow-on Action Recommendations

A report that can be used as input to the process of creating a Business Case/Project Mandate for any follow-on PRINCE2 project and for recording any follow-on instructions covering incomplete products or outstanding issues. It also sets out proposals for post-project review of the project's products.

Gantt Chart

This is a graphic representation of a plan's activities against a time background, showing start and end times and resources required.

Gate Review

A generic term, rather than a PRINCE2 term, meaning a point at the end of a stage or phase where a decision is made whether to continue with the project. In PRINCE2 this would equate to an End Stage Assessment.

Highlight Report

A report from the project manager to the Project Board on a time-driven frequency on stage progress.

Host Organisation

The organisation which owns the project.

Initiation Stage

The first management stage of any PRINCE2 project. Developing information of quality, controls, Project Plan and assembling the Project Initiation Document (PID).

Initiation Stage Plan

A plan, which details the activity and resources, required for initiating the project.

Issue

See 'Project Issue'.

Issue Log

A log of all Project Issues including requests for change raised during the project, showing details of each issue, its evaluation, what decisions about it have been made and its current status.

Lessons Learned Report

A report that describes the lessons learned in undertaking the project and that includes statistics from the quality control of the project's management products. It is approved by the Project Board and then held centrally for the benefit of future projects.

Management by Exception

A management control where the Project Board only needs to be consulted when a plan is forecast to deviate from its approved constraints.

Management Product

Product which is created as a result of using the PRINCE2 Methodology (i.e. Project Brief, PID, Risk Log, Highlight Report, Work Package etc)

Management Stage

Partitions of a project with key decision points.

Mandate

See 'Project Mandate'.

Next Stage Plan

Collective information in the form of Product Descriptions, activity network, Gantt chart, resource report etc, setting out the detailed activities and required resources for the subsequent management stage to be undertaken.

Off-Specification

Something that should be provided by the project, but currently is not (or is forecast not to be) provided. This might be a missing product or a product not meeting its specification.

Outcome

The term used to describe the totality of what the project is set up to deliver, consisting of all the specialist products. For example, this could be an installed computer system with trained staff to use it, backed up by new working practices and documentation, a refurbished and equipped building with all the staff moved in and working, or it could be a new product launched with a recruited and trained sales and support team in place.

Outline Business Case

Information that describes the justification for setting up a PRINCE2 project during project start-up. See also 'Business Case'.

Peer Review

Peer reviews are specific reviews of a project or any of its products where personnel from within the organisation and/or from other organisations carry out an independent assessment of the project. Peer reviews can be done at any point within a project but are often used at stage-end points.

Phase

A part, section or segment of a project, similar in meaning to a PRINCE2 stage. The key meaning of stage in PRINCE2 terms is the use of management stages, ie, sections of the project to which the Project Board only commits one at a time. A phase might be more connected to a time slice, change of skills required or change of emphasis.

PID

See 'Project Initiation Document'.

PID Workshop

A series of workshops involving the project management team, with the objective of creating a Project Initiation Document which can be presented to the Project Board for authorisation.

Plan

A written representation of a series of tasks leading to an objective(?) See also 'Exception Plan'; 'Initiation Plan'; 'Post-Project Review Plan'; 'Project Plan'; 'Project Quality Plan'; 'Stage Plan'; 'Team Plan'.

Plan Text

Narrative which explains the plan, including constraints on the plan, external dependencies, assumptions made, risks identified and their countermeasures.

Post-Implementation Review

See 'Post-Project Review'.

Post-Project Review

One or more reviews held after project closure to determine if the expected benefits have been obtained. Also known as post-implementation review.

Post-Project Review Plan

A plan for the Post-Project Review, which is created within the project life cycle (CP2). The actual review will take place later outside the project life cycle. See 'Post-Project Review'.

PRINCE2

A method that supports some selected aspects of project management.

The acronym stands for PRojects IN Controlled Environments.

PRINCE2 project
A project whose product(s) can be defined at its start sufficiently precisely so as to be measurable against predefined metrics and that is managed according to the PRINCE2 method.

Process
That which must be done to bring about a particular outcome, in terms of information to be gathered, decisions to be made and results that must be achieved.

Producer
This role represents the creator(s) of a product that is the subject of a quality review. Typically, it will be filled by the person who has produced the product or who has led the team responsible.

Product
Any input to or output from a project. PRINCE2 distinguishes between management products (which are produced as part of the management or quality processes of the project) and specialist products (which are those products that make up the final deliverable). A product may itself be a collection of other products.

Product-Based Planning
A three-step diagrammatic technique leading to a comprehensive plan based on creation and delivery of required outputs. The technique considers prerequisite products, quality requirements and the dependencies between products.

Product Breakdown Structure
A hierarchy of all the products to be produced during a plan.

Product Checklist

A list of the major products of a plan, plus key dates in their delivery.

Product Description

A description of a product's purpose, composition, derivation and quality criteria. It is produced at planning time, as soon as the need for the product is identified.

Product Flow Diagram

A diagram showing the sequence of production and interdependencies of the products listed in a Product Breakdown Structure.

Programme

A portfolio of projects selected, planned and managed in a co-ordinated way.

Programme Management

The senior group involved with the overall strategic direction of an organisation (ie, board of directors, partners, strategy committee)

Project

A temporary organisation that is created for the purpose of delivering one or more business products according to a specified Business Case.

Project Approach

A management product which defines how the solution will be delivered (ie, contract out, buy-in, develop existing product, etc.)

Project Assurance

A role for which the Project Board is responsible to assure the management of the project is being conducted properly.

Project Board

The senior management group who have ultimate responsibility for the project.

Project Brief

A description of what the project is to do; a refined and extended version of the Project Mandate, which has been agreed by the Project Board and which is input to project initiation.

Project Closure Notification

Advice from the Project Board to inform the host location that the project resources can be disbanded and support services, such as space, equipment and access, demobilised.

Project Closure Recommendation

Notification prepared by the project manager for the Project Board to send (when the board is satisfied that the project can be closed) to any organisation that has supplied facilities to the project.

Project Initiation Document (PID)

A logical document that brings together the key information needed to start the project on a sound basis and to convey that information to all concerned with the project.

Project Issue

A term used to cover any of the following: a general issue, query, a Request for Change, suggestion or Off-Specification raised during a project. Project Issues can be about anything to do with the project.

Project Management

The planning, monitoring and control of all aspects of the project and the motivation of all those involved in it to achieve the project objectives on time and to the specified cost, quality and performance.

Project Management Team

A term to represent the entire management structure of Project Board, project manager, plus any team manager, Project Assurance and Project Support roles.

Project manager

The person given the authority and responsibility to manage the project on a day-to-day basis to deliver the required products within the constraints agreed with the Project Board.

Project Mandate

Information created externally to the project, which forms the terms of reference and is used to start up the PRINCE2 project.

Project Plan

A high-level plan showing the major products of the project, when they will be delivered and at what cost. An initial Project Plan is presented as part of the Project Initiation Document. This is revised as information on actual progress appears. It is a major control document for the Project Board to measure actual progress against expectations.

Project Quality Plan

A plan defining the key quality criteria, quality control and audit processes to be applied to project management and specialist work in the PRINCE2 project. It will be part of the text in the Project Initiation Document.

Project Records

A collection of all approved management, specialist and quality products and other material, which is necessary to provide an auditable record of the project. NB: This does not include working files.

Project Start-Up Notification

Advice to the host location that the project is about to start and requesting any required Project Support services.

Project Support Office

A service providing administrative services to the project manager. It often provides its services to many projects in parallel.

QMS

See 'Quality Management System'.

Quality

The totality of features and characteristics of a product or service that bear on its ability to satisfy stated and implied needs. Also defined as 'fitness for purpose' or 'conforms to requirements'.

Quality Criteria

A list of criteria that a product must meet in order to pass a quality review and be classed as a 'quality product'. The quality criteria should be specified in the Product Description.

Quality Management System

The complete set of quality standards, procedures and responsibilities for a site or organisation.

Quality Plan

See 'Project Quality Plan'.

Quality Review

A quality review is a quality-checking technique with a specific structure, defined roles and procedure designed to ensure a product's completeness and adherence to standards. The participants are drawn from those with an interest in the product and those with the necessary skills to review its correctness. An example of the checks made by a quality review is 'Does the document match the quality criteria in the Product Description?'

Quality System
See 'Quality Management System'.

Records
See 'Project Records'

Report
Usually a written description of some aspect of the project given to an interested party. See 'Checkpoint Report'; 'End Stage Report'; 'End Project Report'; 'Exception Report'; 'Highlight Report'; 'Lessons Learned Report'.

Request for Change
A means of proposing a modification to the current specification of a product. It is one type of a Project Issue.

Resources Report
A tabular summary of effort, cost and other resource information indicating the planned and actual resource usage for each stage.

Reviewer
A person asked to review a product that is the subject of a quality review.

Risk
The chance of exposure to the adverse or positive consequence of future events.

Risk Analysis

Identification of the importance of each risk, and assignment of owners to 'keep an eye' on each of the risks identified. Responses should also be identified for each risk and any activity needed to manage the risk should be recorded. See 'Risk Management'.

Risk Log

A document that provides identification, estimation, impact evaluation and countermeasures for all risks to the project. It should be created during the start-up of the project and developed during the life of the project. Also known as 'Risk Register'.

Risk Management

Planning and resourcing the activities that need to be undertaken in order to keep identified risks under control. Also monitoring and controlling those activities daily.

Risk Profile

A graphical representation of information normally found on the Risk Log.

Risk Register

See 'Risk Log'.

Roles and Responsibilities

Details of allocated responsibilities for each person appointed to the project. See Appendix B of the PRINCE2 Manual for more details.

Scope

Identification of what will be included within the remit of the project. This should be recorded in the project Brief.

Senior Responsible Owner

This is not a PRINCE2 term, but is used in many organisations. Its equivalent in PRINCE2 terms would be 'Executive'. See also 'Executive'.

Senior Supplier

The Project Board role that provides knowledge and experience of the main discipline(s) involved in the production of the project's deliverable(s). Represents the interests of supplier(s) within the project and provides supplier resources.

Senior User

A member of the Project Board, accountable for ensuring that user needs are specified correctly and that the solution meets those needs.

Sensitivity Analysis

Detailed examination of the impacts of various approaches, solutions and options. Of particular use when establishing whether a project is reliant on one particular benefit over another.

Specialist Product

Products (or deliverables) which represent the end product that will be used for operational purposes.

Sponsor

Not a specific PRINCE2 role but often used to mean the major driving force of a project. May be the equivalent of Executive or corporate/programme management.

Stage

See 'Management Stage'; see also 'Technical Stage'.

Stage Plan

Collective information in the form of Product Descriptions, activity network, Gantt chart, resources report etc, setting out the detailed activities and required resources for a management stage to be undertaken and completed.

Stakeholders

Parties with an interest in the execution and outcome of a project. They would include business streams affected by, or dependent on, the outcome of a project.

Supplier

The group or groups responsible for the supply of the project's specialist products.

Support Office

See 'Project Support Office'.

Team manager

A role undertaken to manage project teams for the project manager.

Team Plan

A detailed plan of activities assigned to the team members.

Technical Stage

The use of a particular set of specialist skills.

Tolerance

The permissible deviation above and below a plan's estimate of time and cost without escalating the deviation to the next level of management. Separate tolerance figures should be given for time and cost. There may also be tolerance levels for quality, scope, benefit and risk. Tolerance is applied at project, stage and team levels.

User(s)

The person or group who will use the final deliverable(s) of the project.

Work Package

The set of information relevant to the creation of one or more products. It will contain the Product Description(s); details of any constraints on production, such as time and cost; interfaces; and confirmation of the agreement between the project manager and the person or team manager who is to implement the Work Package that the work can be done within the constraints.

Work Package Authorisation

The passing of a Work Package from the project manager to the team manager.

Useful contacts

PRINCE User Group (PUG)
c/o Intracite Limited, Murrells House, 6 Murrells Lane,
Frimley Road, Camberley, Surrey GU15 2PY
Telephone: 0870 901 5583 (UK national rates)
Fax: 0870 901 6581
Email: pug@mcmail.com
Website: www.pug.mcmail.com

Professional services, accreditation and examinations
The APM Group Limited
7/8 Queen Square, High Wycombe, Buckinghamshire HP11 2BP
Telephone: 01494 452 450
Fax: 01494 459 559
Email: info@apmgroup.co.uk
Website: www.apmgroup.co.uk

Project Manager Today
![PUBLICATIONS]

Project Manager Today Publications specialises in books and journals related to project management. Titles include:

- *Managing Smaller Projects*
- *Managing Programmes of Business Change*
- *The Programme & Project Support Office Handbook*
- *Managing Risk for Projects and Programmes*

and the flagship monthly magazine:
- *Project Manager Today*

Due for publication in 2003:
- *An Encyclopedia of Project Management*

Publishers of
- *The Cost Engineer*
on behalf of The Association of Cost Engineers

Full details from:
Project Manager Today Publications
Unit 12, Moor Place Farm, Plough Lane, Bramshill, Hook
Hampshire
RG27 0RF

Tel: 0118 932 6665
Fax: 0118 932 6663
Email: info@projectmanagertoday.co.uk
Website: www.pmtoday.co.uk

Project Manager Today also organises topical conferences and seminars.